Unbuttoned

Unbuttoned: The Art and Artists of Theatrical Costume Design documents the creative journey as costumes develop from concept to performance. Each chapter provides an overview of the process, including designing and shopping; draping, cutting, dyeing, and painting; and beading, sewing, and creating embellishments and accessories. This book features interviews with practitioners from Broadway and regional theaters to opera and ballet companies, offering valuable insights into the costume design profession. Exceptional behind-the-scenes photography illustrates top costume designers and craftspeople at work, along with gorgeous costumes in progress.

E. Shura Pollatsek is a professional costume designer for stage and screen, an Associate Professor of Costume Design and Technology, and an award-winning author of several nationally published articles. She designs costumes for performances across the United States and internationally, and for National PBS television and Showtime. During a decade based in New York City, she worked for Off Broadway and Broadway productions, the Metropolitan Opera, and at many leading regional theaters.

Mitchell D. Wilson is a National Press Photographer of the Year winner who travels the world capturing time and place in stills and motion. His work has also been recognized with Primetime Emmys, both the DuPont Columbia Award and the Peabody for Excellence in Broadcast Journalism, two International Documentary Association Awards for Best Documentary Series, and many others. He began his career as a Combat Cameraman and underwater photographer in the elite Combat Camera Group of the U.S. Navy.

For more information, please visit shuracostumedesign.com and mitchelldwilson.com

Unbuttoned

The Art and Artists of Theatrical Costume Design

E. Shura Pollatsek

Photography by Mitchell D. Wilson

Routledge
Taylor & Francis Group

NEW YORK AND LONDON

First published 2017
by Routledge
711 Third Avenue, New York, NY, 10017

and by Routledge
2 Park Square, Milton Park, Abingdon, Oxon OX14 4RN

Routledge is an imprint of the Taylor & Francis Group, an informa business

Library of Congress Cataloging in Publication Data
Names: Pollatsek, Shura, author.
Title: Unbuttoned : the art and artists of theatrical costume design /
Shura Pollatsek.
Description: New York : Routledge/Taylor & Francis Group, 2016. |
Includes bibliographical references and index.
Identifiers: LCCN 2015038712| ISBN 9781138919037 (pbk. : alk. paper) |
ISBN 9781315688084 (ebook : alk. paper)
Subjects: LCSH: Costume.
Classification: LCC PN2067 .P65 2016 | DDC 792.02/6—dc23
LC record available at http://lccn.loc.gov/2015038712

ISBN: 978-1-138-91903-7 (pbk)
ISBN: 978-1-315-68808-4 (ebk)

All photography by Mitchell D. Wilson

Typeset in Slimbach and Helvetica
By Keystroke, Station Road, Codsall, Wolverhampton

Printed and bound in India by Replika Press Pvt. Ltd.

Table of Contents

Acknowledgments   vii
Biographies   ix

Introduction   xi

Chapter 1   Design   1
Creating the Vision   1
The Bold Colorist—Richard Hudson   3
A Passion for Collaboration—Julie Scobeltzine   7
Revealing Characters—Fabio Toblini   8
Continually Exploring—David C. Woolard   12
Bringing It All Together—Alain Germain   17

Chapter 2   Sourcing Materials   21
Filling in the Outlines   21
Supporting the Design—Shopper Sarah Bahr   28
A Library of Textiles—Eduardo Madrid At B&J Fabrics   33
Supplying the Choices—Purchasing Manager Tim Blacker   38

Chapter 3   Draping and Cutting   43
Sculpting the Shape   43
Costume Architect—Kjersten Lester-Moratzka   50
Transforming Bodies—Triffin Morris   57
Translating the Sketch—David Arevalo   62

Chapter 4   Fabric Embellishment   69
Creating a Custom Surface   69
Lizards and Cats—Painter Parmelee Tolkan   74
From Traditional to Digital—Painter-Dyer Caroline Dignes   80
Sparkle and Texture—Bead Manager Polly Isham Kinney   85

Chapter 5   **Construction   91**

Building the Garment   91

Couture and Stage—Costumer Quentin Desfray   95

A Love of Sewing—Stitcher Louisa Williams   103

Part of the Process—First Hand Ashley Rigg   108

Chapter 6   **Crafts and Millinery   117**

Creating Accessories   117

Testing the Molds—Milliner Arnold Levine   120

Drilling and Melting—The Crafts Department At
    Parsons-Meares, Ltd.   125

Hats, Headdresses, and Helmets—Milliner Deborah Nash   128

Leather as a Medium—Craftsman Yann Boulet   134

Building Masks, Building Relationships—Craftsman Brian Russman   138

Chapter 7   **Wigs and Hair   147**

Finishing the Look   147

Rotating Repertory—David Zimmerman   151

The Danger of Live Performance—Christine "Micki" Chomicki   156

Finding the Context—Heather Fleming   163

Chapter 8   **Putting It All Together   169**

Creating a Character   169

Acknowledgments

Thank you to all of the costume shops, studios, and other venues that made time for us to visit and capture images while researching this book: Any D'Avray, Arnold S. Levine Inc., Atelier Caraco Canezou, B&J Fabrics, Barbara Matera Ltd., Butterfly Fabrics, Compagnie Alain Germain, Custom Wig Company, Daytona Trimming, M&J Trimmings, Mine Barral Vergez, Parsons-Meares Ltd., Rodney Gordon Inc., The Santa Fe Opera Costume Shop, Textile Fabrics, Tricorne Studios, and Les Vertugadins. I am grateful to all of the designers, artisans, and others who shared their stories, talents, and artistry. It was such a treat to have the opportunity to sit down with both longtime colleagues and new friends and discuss this crazy, wonderful field of ours. I also owe a big thank you to the designers, directors, choreographers, and technicians I have worked with over the years who might recognize their work in my examples and anecdotes.

I appreciate those who gave both personal and professional support during the development, writing, and completion of this book: friends and family who read drafts and gave feedback, or cheered us on in other ways; the WKU Office of Research and Sponsored Programs that funded much of the travel required to research the book; my colleagues in the WKU Department of Theatre and Dance for their encouragement and for managing without me while I was on sabbatical; the editors and staff at Focal Press who helped us to shape the manuscript. I also want to acknowledge *Theatre Design & Technology* magazine, which published two articles that served as a preliminary exploration of this topic of creative collaboration, and gave me the foundation for pursuing a book-length project.

But most of all, I would like to thank my collaborator on this project: my husband Mitch. You are my inspiration, best friend, favorite travel companion and true love. You have taught me about light and shadow, keen observation, and breaking for happy hour. I am incapable of writing the thousands and thousands of words your eloquent pictures are worth.

E. Shura Pollatsek is a versatile designer whose work spans theater, dance, opera, film, and television. She has designed costumes for performances across the United States and internationally, and for National PBS television and Showtime. During a decade based in New York City, she worked for Off Broadway and Broadway productions, the Metropolitan Opera, and at many leading regional theaters.

Shura holds an MFA in Costume Design from New York University's Tisch School of the Arts and is a proud member of United Scenic Artists Local 829. She travels internationally, speaks fluent French, and dabbles in textile art. After many years as a freelance artist, she is now based in Kentucky, where she is an Associate Professor of Costume Design and Technology at WKU. In addition to teaching, she maintains an active design career. She has published three articles in national magazines, one of which won the Herbert Greggs Merit Award. This is her first book.

Mitchell D. Wilson is well known for cinematic eloquence, impressionistic historical re-creations, and striking juxtaposition of photojournalism and visual metaphor. He has traveled the world capturing time and place in stills and motion. His striking photos are collected in books and have been exhibited in galleries. He was both cinematographer and co-director for the eight-hour, award-winning series *The Great War and the Shaping of the Twentieth Century*. Other favorite projects that he co-directed and filmed include *The New Heroes*, hosted by Robert Redford, *The Kingdom of David, Andrew Jackson: Good, Evil and the Presidency* and the four-hour PBS history of aviation project *Chasing the Sun*. His impressive credits also include several programs for The American Experience, PBS' preeminent history series, including the three-hour Woodrow Wilson Presidential special, and *The Duel*.

His creative talents have also been widely showcased on ABC, NBC, CBS, and HBO. An Ernie Crisp National Press Photographer of the Year winner, his work has also been recognized with Primetime Emmys, the DuPont Columbia Award, the Peabody Award for Excellence in Broadcast Journalism, two International Documentary Association Awards, and many others. He began his career as a Combat Cameraman and underwater photographer in the elite Combat Camera Group of the U.S. Navy. He is a member of the Directors Guild of America.

For more information, please visit shuracostumedesign.com and mitchelldwilson.com

Introduction

Popular culture tends to show two versions of making clothing: mass-production drudgery in sweatshops, or virtually instantaneous bursts of creative magic. The princess in *Enchanted* turns curtains overnight into an eye-catching floral dress (and also seems well rested); Catwoman makes a curve-hugging jumpsuit complete with stiletto-heeled boots out of a rain slicker. They don't use patterns; they just cut shapes out of the fabric. Everything fits perfectly on the first try.

Making custom clothing for the stage can seem magical. It is just as magical as the way flour and yeast, when combined with the right amount of elbow grease, become a delicious, crusty loaf of bread. Most people do not see the planning and time that the transformation of fabric into wearable art entails. Creating costumes actually requires a combination of art, craft, and engineering. Outfits for actors are chosen more precisely than ordinary clothing—designers pick styles that help communicate the story to the audience. Technicians construct stage costumes to fit well and add visual flair to the production. They ensure that sashes stay tied in perfect bows and vests never ride up to reveal a gap of shirt below. Those in the industry typically refer to the work as building clothing rather than making it, and with good reason. Even costumes that look like ordinary clothing are specialized beneath the surface. Everything from gossamer silks to finely tailored suits may have to endure fighting, dancing, or fast changes, eight shows a week.

Very few people in modern society make clothing beyond tie dyeing a T-shirt or adapting a shawl into a beach cover-up. Costume shops are some of the last places where the creation of custom handcrafted garments is widely practiced. Unlike the mass-market fashion industry, which designs and makes clothes for generic and idealized body-types, costumes are created precisely for each individual, as well as over bodies altered by padding, corsets, or hoopskirts. Nothing can be mass-produced. Even a set of matching dresses for a chorus must be calibrated so that each skirt ends at the same distance off the floor, and each neckline shows the same amount of collarbone.

Most people understand that patterning and sewing professionally require training and talent, and that designers need a great eye for line, shape, and color. The less

Finishing touches are put on a green leather jacket for the opera *Carmen* at the Santa Fe Opera.

Dress forms stand guard in the hallway at Atelier Caraco Canezou in Paris.

Tailor François Simeon at work at Atelier Caraco Canezou in Paris.

obvious skill is the constant creative problem solving. Certainly there are times when the cleverness of the costume department is on display, such as when Cinderella makes an onstage transformation from rags to a ball gown, or Cleopatra suddenly sprouts a set of gleaming gold wings. However, most of the innovation happens on a smaller scale. The creative thinking is so embedded in an ordinary day's work that those in the practice barely notice they are doing it. Sometimes the innovations are to save time, such as adding decorative tucks to make a vintage dress fit the actor, rather than doing a more time-consuming "proper" alteration involving removing and replacing the zipper.

Time is a factor in summer stock where they put up several large shows in a month, but also on Broadway, where scenes may be rewritten only weeks before opening night. Ingenuity is also called for to stretch a budget. Often costumers find clever substitutes for expensive materials, or try to make do with what they have on hand. They might figure out the jigsaw puzzle of making a dress from the 5-½-yard piece of fabric on the sale table when the pattern really needed 6. And of course, creative problem solving is needed to invent something never before seen—post-apocalyptic armor for Scottish clansmen, or a dress that conceals a rolling chair so the wearer can glide across the stage.

Crafts Artisan Bryant Villasana painting sculptural masks for *Le Rossignol* at the Santa Fe Opera.

Another striking aspect of the costume industry is the constant collaboration. The problem solving rarely happens alone at the drawing board. Instead it happens when hashing out ideas with collaborators in meetings, or in the workroom, experimenting with combinations of materials. As the designers and artisans interviewed for this book shared their stories, the pronoun most commonly used was "we." "We figured out the best dye process," "we decided to make the hats out of felt instead of leather." Technicians often credited the designer's sketch with inspiring a new technique, and designers were quick to mention how a wonderful draper or crafts artisan had breathed life into an idea they were not completely sure how to bring to the stage.

I was inspired to write this book after some years as a professor of costume design and technology. In my earlier career as a costume designer in New York, I was aware I had an interesting and unusual job. One friend in particular loved to call me and ask where I was. The answer might be choosing colorful acrylic rods at Canal Plastics in Chinatown or searching the photo archives at Ellis Island. However, I did not spend much time reflecting upon the field of costuming as a practice until I became a professor. Teaching causes one to look at a familiar topic from an outsider's point of view, and I began to see how unusual and fascinating many processes were that I took for granted. As I gathered compelling stories and philosophies

A close-up of an industrial iron.

from those interviewed for this book, my appreciation of the field's unique qualities continued to grow.

Our intention with this book is to illuminate how each artisan plays a role as a costume progresses from initial conception to the performance onstage. We focus on neither the design nor the finished costume, but rather the creative journey as the clothing takes shape.

The costume designer and the costume makers solve problems collaboratively to make a sculpture out of fabric that fulfills the vision of the sketch, and comes to life on the stage. Through personal stories and unique behind-the-scenes photography, the reader will get a close look not only at the garments created for the stage, but also at the individuals who make this distinctive art their life's work.

Design

CREATING THE VISION

For the costume makers, whose work we explore in this book, the process starts with the costume design sketch. For the costume designer, the journey begins with a script and a vision. Unlike a fashion designer, for whom the clothing is the end product, a costume designer's product is actually the character. The clothing helps to illuminate the social role and personality of each member of the story. The visual tableau created by the combination of characters onstage gives insight into the plot and themes of the performance. The context of every costume is extremely important. Designers create each look for a specific performer playing a specific role at a specific moment in a story. A full skirt might be designed so that the stiff fabric will sway and snap when the actress does her choreography, or the actor's clownish interpretation of his role might inspire a too-tight suit jacket and bright tie. When costumes are successful, the designer's role is imperceptible. Instead, the clothing becomes a natural part of the character onstage.

Designer Alain Germain pages through a book of his designs.

Germain with an original painting at his studio in Paris.

Design for the stage is a collaborative art, led by the director. Costume designers work as part of a creative team of artists. This production team, comprised of scenic, lighting, sound, and costume designers, meets with the director and/or choreographer to discuss the story and to find a vision for the particular production. The director shares his or her initial thoughts, and then after a group discussion, the designers begin their own explorations, looking for a way to translate the ideas to the stage. Most start with research into the era and style of the piece, many readings of the script, and listening to music if there is any. Over a series of meetings, they discard many sketches and rework countless ideas. Finally the costume designs evolve into finished color paintings, called renderings. However, the designer's work is not done yet. As the actors rehearse with the director, their interpretations of their roles may inspire adjustments, large or small, to the designs. And as costumes enter the construction phase, the collaboration also continues. The best costume technicians do not merely execute the design; they add their own artistry as they interpret it, much as musicians playing from printed sheet music produce their unique version of a song.

The designer has a series of meetings with those who will source the materials, make the patterns, dye the fabrics, and sculpt the accessories. As the costume technologists look at the renderings, they ask the designer logistical questions. What kind of fabric is the dress made from? How does the coat open? Does the performer remove the mask onstage? The production team is now armed to start work, but they continue to check in periodically with the designer as they build. Rough draft, or "mock-up" versions are made first, and most garments are fitted on the performer in multiple sessions, giving both designer and artisan a chance to make aesthetic and practical adjustments.

Fittings are a critical phase of a designer's work. The costume a designer sees in her mind as she draws is not a fully realized idea. No matter how experienced the designer, nor how detailed the sketch, the three-dimensional garment on the moving, breathing performer brings up new questions and demands adjustments. Maybe the hemline looks better on the actress above the knee than below, now that the fight scene the director added necessitated a change from heels to flats. Maybe the pant leg needs to be a bit narrower than was fashionable in the 1930s to keep the actor from seeming frumpy to the modern eye. Maybe the wings protrude at the wrong angle from the dancer's back once she has done a few pirouettes. The fitting is also a chance to see the whole costume together: the clothing, the hat, the shoes, and even the wig. While additional fine-tuning will occur during dress rehearsals, everyone prefers to first work out as many kinks as possible in the relative calm of the costume shop.

Just because a show has opened on Broadway does not mean the designer's job is done. When a Broadway show goes on tour, the overall look of the show remains the same, but the set, costume, and lighting designers adjust their original visions to be portable, and of a slightly more modest scale. Martin Pakledinaz was tasked with reworking his original costume designs for *Thoroughly Modern Millie* into an efficient touring package. He cut a few of the outfits for the leading ladies. Plenty of glamor remained, though—the title character still wore seven dresses every evening. His greatest change was to give the members of the chorus a more modular look. Instead of a complete new outfit for each of the big numbers, they changed jackets, hats, and accessories to shift from people on the street to speakeasy revelers to high society party guests. To ensure that the color combinations in this new version would still create a dynamic yet balanced stage picture, Pakledinaz's assistants made a poster-sized chart. Along the side was a list of all the characters and along the top were the dozens of scenes in the show. Each box in the grid represented a character in a given scene. The assistants filled each box with small pieces of the fabrics that made up the costume, such as a larger patch of the suit fabric, a small square of shirt color, and a sliver of tie. Using the chart, the designer could see the entire show at once without covering the office in a blanket of costume sketches. The designer and director could easily discuss the sequence of outfits for one character, or see the grouping of printed silks in a dance number. Pakledinaz checked that there was never a moment where too much of one color was used, or a scene where Millie did not stand out as she should. Despite having won the Tony Award for his Broadway design, Pakledinaz decided afterwards that he preferred the streamlined look of the tour.

THE BOLD COLORIST—RICHARD HUDSON

Richard Hudson is a costume and scenic designer with a distinguished career in theater, opera, and ballet design. He is probably best known for his scenic design for *The Lion King*, which won numerous awards including the Tony. Hudson grew up in what is now Zimbabwe (then Southern Rhodesia) "in the middle of the bush." His interest in performance was sparked as he and his siblings created their own entertainment. "One of my greatest passions when I was tiny was puppets, and doing puppet shows," he recalls. "I think that is what first engendered my enthusiasm for the theater." Later Hudson made his actual theater debut at boarding school, where the students presented plays. He made his contribution off-stage, by painting the scenery. At the age of eighteen he left Africa for London, where he attended the Wimbledon School of Art. "Certainly one of the things I love most about my job is the collaboration. That's really what it's all about, right from the beginning of the project, when working with a director or a choreographer discussing what they feel about the piece. . . . Of course it's not just a question of collaborating with the drapers and the people who are making the costumes, but quite often talking to the people who are going to wear them. I do quite a lot of opera, and often work with big opera stars. It's obviously part of my job to talk to them about what they are going to wear."

The American Ballet Theatre in New York City is presenting a new production of *The Nutcracker* at the Brooklyn Academy of Music, with scenery and costumes by Richard Hudson. For this production

Designer Richard Hudson painting at Barbara Matera Ltd. costume shop.

of the beloved Christmas ballet, choreographer Alexei Ratmansky requested a traditional style, but Hudson's designs will have a distinctly different look than the classic New York City Ballet production, costumes designed by Barbara Karinska in 1954. Hudson chose to set the first act in the early nineteenth century, with a Northern European feel. Before he puts pen to paper, Hudson fills a file with research. Costume designers typically gather images from the time such as fashion illustrations, paintings, and photographs of vintage garments. For the second act, when the ballet takes us to the "Land of Sweets," he switches gears. Hudson, known for his distinctive and bold use of color, has carefully plotted out tableaux of "very brightly colored" costumes against more abstracted settings. "The Arabian girls are dark red and gold, the flowers in 'The Waltz of the Flowers' are quite bright pink. The set for the second act is a turquoise surround with a lime yellow. And then it changes right at the end of the second act, for the *pas de deux* to, sort of a deep purply blue."

Hudson puts finishing touches on his designs for American Ballet Theatre's production of *The Nutcracker*.

Hudson and Tim Blacker at Barbara Matera costume shop in New York.

Once Hudson is satisfied with his research, he tries out ideas in a sketchbook, and then finally draws and paints his finished renderings. The paintings show the overall look of the costume, but as he meets with the costume shop, they will also refer to research and detail sketches, for the paintings cannot contain all of the information. Experienced pattern makers will already be familiar with the historical shapes, but the designer's research helps to show them which nuances and variations of the period he prefers. To convey the exact shapes of the embroidery for Clara's bodice, he included both a detail drawing and a photo of the scrollwork on an antique mirror that inspired him. Despite having such a specific vision of his work, Hudson "loves it when people make suggestions. I am not autocratic. I love the collaborative process and the fact that everybody chips in. I think the best projects are ones where you can't remember who thought of what. It all comes together."

The London-based Hudson is spending time in New York to coordinate with the shops hard at work translating his designs into clothing and scenery. His clear sketches and binder of research give the costumers at Barbara Matera Ltd. an excellent starting point, but the translation to three dimensions still requires input from the designer. Hudson will meet with the shoppers to select fabrics and trimmings for each element of each costume, discuss silhouette and proportion with the pattern makers, and finesse fit and shape on the individual performers. The lines and swirls in his sketches will be translated into embellishments like beading, embroidery, and painting, and he will work closely with the artisans as they sample techniques and colors. However, the costumes won't be truly finalized until dress rehearsal, when Hudson will witness his creations in their full context: onstage, in motion, under colored stage lights. Then he, together with choreographer Ratmansky, will critique the look of the show. The designer will have his final chance to edit, and will ensure that hem lengths are adjusted, paint colors are brightened, and earrings with more sparkle are added before audiences see the ballet.

A PASSION FOR COLLABORATION—
JULIE SCOBELTZINE

Parisian costume designer Julie Scobeltzine fell into her career rather than planning it, although naturally careers often diverge from formal training. Her teachers from her graduate study in scenic design told her that out of the dozen students in a class, two would actually wind up working in the field. She agrees with the assessment. "I have a classmate who does store windows for high end jewelry, one who does illustrations, another who is a director. Everyone does different things, and I do costumes. One or two actually do set design." In fact, although the majority of her career has been in costumes, she has begun designing both scenery and costumes for some of her shows.

Scobeltzine's entry into the costume design field was something of a fluke. A year after graduation from the École Nationale Supérieure des Arts Décoratifs, she sought an opportunity to broaden her training. She asked a classmate who was working as the assistant scenic designer on a production who the costume designer was, and if they might need an intern. Scobeltzine loved fabric, and had dabbled in making accessories, but her experience stopped there, so she was floored when she was asked to be the costume designer. The original costume designer had walked out on the project, and the set designer, who was her former professor, thought she was up to the task. She was frank about her inexperience, but she "had a meeting and no one asked me if I did or didn't want to do it." To implement the show, a (non-Disney) *Beauty and the Beast* musical that included ice skaters, she was given a budget from which to hire staff and buy supplies. With help from her experienced support staff, "I learned how to do all of it. How to run a shop, do fittings, find a team to do makeup and hair, manage the money. I really loved it, and I found I had a passion for it."

Now well into her career, designing for major theaters and opera companies throughout Europe, Scobeltzine has a good understanding of sewing, patterning, and choosing fabrics, but she still prefers to work with costume shops that don't merely execute designs. "The relationship with the costume makers is very important . . . I understand sewing techniques . . . and I can suggest different cuts, but I prefer collaborators who are spirited, and make suggestions. Better things happen when you work as a team." A project whose success she credits to teamwork was a production of *Titus Andronicus* at Théâtre de Gennevilliers. She wanted to use something as similar as possible to real Roman togas, and did extensive research into the intricacies of the drapery, and how different wearers personalized them according to taste, station, and age. "In Roman times, people knew how to pleat them, how to wear them. Today of course we are incapable of this. I can't ask [the actors] to spend a month learning how to wear something. So, we had to invent a toga that would stay on the body, but give the impression of being authentic." The draper, in charge of patterning, proposed several ideas, and gradually they settled on a pleated skirt with two long streamers attached that could be wound around the body in various configurations. The draper wanted to make the pleats and folds more set and secured, and the designer wanted them to look more natural, but eventually they found a solution that satisfied everyone, including the actors.

Working at the Burgtheater in Vienna was a complete contrast. Despite the prestigious resume credit and the plentiful budget, she found the process of putting up a show there painful. The workroom held nearly 100 employees. "There was everything—people making hats and shoes. It was like a little factory—everyone was in white smocks and no one spoke." The head of the shop asked her to specify every detail, down to how many centimeters long a sleeve was, rather than letting the drapers and tailors interpret the sketches for themselves. Scobeltzine found the meetings tedious, and she felt that the costume makers did too. Although working through an interpreter, Scobeltzine understood enough German to catch two stitchers griping about making vents in a lightweight tunic. The designer told them she wanted their feedback, as they had much more experience finishing clothes. "I thought [the slits] would look pretty and they were in my drawing, but if you think that it won't work in this fabric, please tell me!" Despite Scobeltzine's plea, the head of the shop made clear that the employees' input was not welcome.

Designer Fabio Toblini in a fitting with dancer Xiaoxiao Wang, who plays the Mechanical Bird in *Le Rossignol* at the Santa Fe Opera.

REVEALING CHARACTERS—FABIO TOBLINI

Fabio Toblini stands in the fitting room, considering a petite dancer clad in a metallic gold body suit. Sculptural flanges protrude from her hips, giving the look of armor. The designer studies the lines of her body in the mirror, deciding the most pleasing proportion on her delicate frame. Should the flange sit a bit lower on the tailbone? Should it hug the body more or flare at a different angle? The pieces are repositioned and pinned in place, so he can be sure he made the right adjustment. The dancer adds a tall, feathered headpiece, and when she tries a flourish with the matching feather fans, she nearly fills the small room. While she experiments, gauging how the large fans will affect her choreography, Toblini again looks at the whole picture. Does the sweep of the headdress feel harmonious with the structure on her hips? Do the lines of the costume show clearly amidst all of the metallic shine?

Toblini grew up in a small town in northern Italy. He didn't have exposure to the arts in school, but at home developed an early interest in clothing. "I was a child who made dresses for my sisters' dolls. My mother got a knitting machine when I was eight, and I learned to use it right away." He studied fashion in Milan and then began work in the industry. That year and a half "was enough for me to know it wasn't where I wanted to be." After an "existential crisis," he

Marking adjustments on the felt cap that will support Wang's headdress.

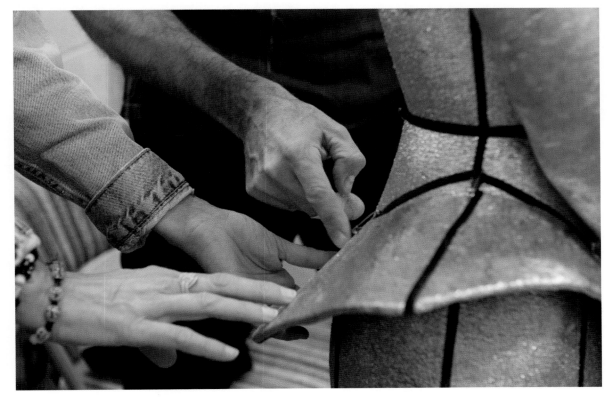

Designer and draper discuss the shape of a panel on the Mechanical Bird costume.

Toblini, Wang, and Assistant Milliner Joanna Koefoed check the fit of the cap that when finished will look like a stylized hairstyle.

explains with a wry smile at his younger self, he left Italy for England and enrolled at a Waldorf school for adults, studying an array of arts. He gravitated toward singing, and moved to Hamburg, Germany, to pursue further studies in voice. At the school, the students presented an opera, and the former fashion designer was pressed into service for the costumes. While he had thought he never wanted to do anything with clothes again, "it was a total revelation because conceptually it [costumes] is the opposite of fashion. The problem I had with fashion was that . . . I had to cover up and create this fake, phony image . . . I felt like I was doing a total disservice to humanity." Once he started working on the costumes for the opera,

he realized that rather than using clothes to conceal his own nature, he was "trying to find an image to reveal as much of [the characters] as possible and I thought 'Oh my god! This is it, this is it!"

Soon after this realization, Toblini came to New York City on a whim. He knew nothing about theater but he did know a lot about clothing. And so, he found his way to Izquierdo Studio where he performed a variety of jobs, including stitching, distressing, and painting. At the shop Toblini made connections with costume designers who were clients, and after a time he was able to transition to assistant design work. "I was so lacking in knowledge of theater but I knew a lot about fabrics, about the cut, what crosses over from fashion design to theater,

Toblini watches as Wang tries out the feather fan prototypes.

the technical stuff . . . [the designer] thought he'd have to teach me everything, but from day one I was bringing back all the fabrics that he needed. I was actually useful!" he mentions proudly. After working for several designers, Toblini found a kindred spirit in Catherine Zuber, and assisted her for five years. He became familiar with her methods in all aspects of the design process, and for Toblini, "basically that was my graduate training." After a time, he felt ready to take on his own design projects, and he gradually built a solid career working at major theater, opera, and dance venues around the United States.

Toblini's current project, *Le Rossignol*, is an opera with a Chinese folktale setting. The director, Michael Gieleta, chose to merge the Asian story with the art world of early twentieth-century Paris, the milieu of the opera's composer, Stravinsky. The opera begins in a rehearsal room, where dueling divas drive a director to his breaking point. Suddenly the 1917 world fades away, deconstructing into the fantastical folktale. This gave Toblini free rein to combine a wide variety of influences. In addition to the main source material of Edwardian clothing and works of artists like Picasso and Miro, Toblini threw his research net widely. "I started looking at postmodern 1980s takes on art. I looked at samurais, at Pucci [the fashion designer], structural dresses, kimonos, and . . . I just put it together so it would be as strange as possible."

To effect the onstage transformation from the "real" rehearsal room to the folktale characters, Toblini collaborated with the Santa Fe Opera's costume makers. Although the shifting scenery and swirling projections will provide some distraction, the change needs to be smooth and graceful. The character of the director becomes the Emperor. His shirt, vest, and tie are built as a one-piece garment that will unfasten and come off together. The long jewel-toned Emperor robe is then put on over his suit pants and zipped up. The actress playing the Nightingale will wear her simple Grecian style gown under her Parisian dress, and to change she simply unfastens the top dress, lets it fall to the floor, and steps out. As the folktale starts, she will add an open robe with deep wing-like sleeves. As eye-catching as the costumes may be, Toblini ensures that his work meshes seamlessly with the scenery, projections, choreography, and acting style. "It's coming out really well. Everybody is cross-pollinating. As a designer you have to be sure you are not overwhelming—because it is never about the costumes."

CONTINUALLY EXPLORING—DAVID C. WOOLARD

David C. Woolard began college planning on a career in psychology, and that initial training has served him well in his current career. Once he switched to design, he pursued all areas, but the link to the human psyche caused him to gravitate to costumes. "That training was very helpful for plot analysis and . . . figuring out who these characters are and how they should inhabit themselves." He also found that his desire to look beneath the human surface helped him to work more productively with his colleagues. Sometimes an actor displaces other problems onto the costume. The issue might actually be something from the rehearsal process or stress in their personal life that comes to a head when the actor is standing in front of the fitting room mirror. "It's a really important thing," Woolard explains, "to try to figure out what *they* need and also make sure that *you* are getting your process and your art."

Woolard has practiced his art on Broadway, and at major theater and opera companies around the United States and worldwide. In addition to feeding his interest in psychology, Woolard is drawn to the field of costume design because it gives him the chance to explore. "For every show I design, there is some new interesting problem to solve. There is some new interesting piece of research to deal with. Usually both." Sometimes that problem is working through a character's emotional journey over three acts or combining two aesthetics coherently, but often the challenge involves a physical aspect. He enjoys learning about a new way to texture fabric or figuring

out how to make a costume transform onstage. A typical example from Woolard's career is a production of *A Midsummer Night's Dream* at La Jolla Playhouse. The basis for the costume design came from director Christopher Ashley's central concept that, as Woolard explains, "the court was the Victoriana court, and then the forest is the upside-down world of that court." For his costume design, in addition to having the fairy costumes be imaginative riffs on 1840s clothing worn upside-down, "I wanted to bring into it a very organic feel when we got into the fairy world. I wanted to have it seem that the forest . . . had taken over, that the forest had created the clothes. So, we used a lot of vine, branch, leaf, and flower imagery in the designs."

This production gave Woolard a chance to collaborate not only with the costume makers at La Jolla Playhouse, but also with a custom flower company in New York, M&S Schmalberg. His designs called for the fairies to be accented with leaves, petals, and vines made from fabrics evoking the Victorian setting of the play, not from standard fabric flowers one might purchase ready-made. He had expected to be limited to using stiff fabrics, but he learned that Schmalberg had a way to starch most fabrics to make them compatible. The flower company was able to suggest which fabrics might work best to create each specific shape the designer envisioned. "This was great because it freed me up a lot to use brocades and . . . some of the more Victoriana feeling fabrics that I wanted . . . prints and paisleys." Woolard prowled the workshop, choosing shapes he liked among the antique cast-iron molds in their collection. He enjoyed learning more about the machines that stamped and molded the fabric into naturalistic curled and veined leaves. Once he understood the process, it helped him to figure out how to best adapt the product to his particular set of costumes. He created unique textured fabric collages for the fairies. One had a skirt made of layers of chiffon, sprinkled with petals. For those that did a lot of physical acrobatics, he combined the three-dimensional fabric leaves with flat versions painted directly onto the costume.

The interaction with technicians often spurs Woolard to finesse his designs in ways he had not originally envisioned. For his current project, *Anthony and Cleopatra* at Oregon Shakespeare Festival, he designed a set of lapis and gold wings for Cleopatra when she is dressed as the goddess Isis. He knew he wanted the wings to hang from her arms and unfurl as she raised them, but left the details of the mechanism to the crafts department. Their solution, fastening the feathers to each other so the wings would open like a fan, inspired Woolard. To make the moment yet more theatrical, he had the crafts artisans figure out a way for the last few feathers to be

Cast-iron molds for leaves and flowers at M&S Schmalberg custom flower company in New York.

Above and below: Designer David C. Woolard with his sketches for *A Midsummer Night's Dream* to be performed at La Jolla Playhouse.

controlled by the actress' fingers. This way, when she spread the wings, the tips could arc up into a more dramatic shape.

Woolard finds joy in working with others to create beauty. For another of Cleopatra's gowns, he and the draper who patterned the dress jointly figured out the perfect flattering diagonal seam that enhanced the lines of both the dress and the actress. "Granted, this is an outdoor theater so not many people are going to see this [detail], but it was exciting for me that that was able to happen, and exciting for the draper." The actress felt beautiful and confident, and the dress helped her inhabit the role of the famous Egyptian queen. As a designer, Woolard knows that he serves several masters. He implements the vision of the director. And, "I always feel that there are things that I do for the audience, to help them understand the story of the show, there are things that I do for the actor, and there are things that I do for myself."

Below: A partial view of Woolard's large collection of fabric samples, which hang on the wall.

Right and opposite: Designer Alain Germain at his studio in Paris.

A book of Germain's designs.

BRINGING IT ALL TOGETHER—ALAIN GERMAIN

Alain Germain briskly crosses his charming garret of a studio. His main workspace is two adjoining rooms in a centuries-old building in Paris, the walls lined with framed costume design sketches. Every surface in the outer room is covered with the accumulated artifacts of his four-decade career. Shelves, tables, and even chairs hold books, papers, sculptures, computers, brochures, and posters. The inner room has storage for art supplies but its surfaces are left relatively empty, and tables and drawing boards provide an inviting place to create new works. Germain is reworking a poster from a past produc-

tion, turning it into a collage for an upcoming gallery exhibit. He adds some additional shading using chalk pastels, and then prepares to dissect the paper and rearrange the image into a refracted abstraction.

Germain has designed costumes and scenery for numerous productions in opera and theater over his career, some for other groups, and many for his eponymous company. The Compagnie Alain Germain combines dance, music, theater, and visual art to create genre-spanning works that are sometimes performed in museums rather than in standard theaters. In addition to designing scenery and costumes, Germain also directs and choreographs. For his earliest

Above and opposite: Germain shades with pastels on a poster that will become a part of one of his collage-style artworks.

productions, he pulled together costumes from thrift shop finds. "I transformed things that already existed. I did assemblages. I added a lot. We didn't have money for the productions so it was unthinkable to have things made." However, with the company's success, he transitioned to conceiving the costumes ahead of time, and drew meticulous sketches to be realized by costume shops. Germain always found himself inspired by the range of possibilities in fabric treatments. "I work a lot with textures, with different materials. There are fabrics that don't exist that I invent by collage, burning and etc. to transform them. That's what I like about stage design—since it's seen from a distance everything is possible."

Germain started his training in the arts in piano and dance. With surprising self-awareness for a fifteen-year-old, he saw that although he had talent, he could never be at the level required to succeed

professionally. "I was a decent pianist, a decent dancer, but not great. So my muse was to do other things, and bring it all together. I knew [I was cut out to direct] very early." Germain enrolled in art school, where he studied all areas: sculpture, painting, and interior design. After receiving diplomas in architecture from both the École Nationale Supérieure des Arts Décoratifs and the École Nationale Supérieure des Beaux-Arts, Germain fell right into his first theatrical production. He had an idea, and "knocked on doors" until he found a producer for his multimedia piece. He was given two weeks at the Grand Palais in Paris, an early success that he finds startling in hindsight. With arts funding so much tighter now, such opportunities are sadly unthinkable for young artists these days.

Although Germain is known for his conceptual work, the practical aspect is also very important to him. A costume must not keep a performer from kneeling, dancing, or any physicality the show needs. "For me a stage costume is a work uniform. It's as if you made an outfit for a cook or a chambermaid, but instead it's an actor or a dancer. It has to be very solidly built and also very precise." Even some of his most unusual costumes, such as a classic Citroën 2CV car forming a tortoise-like shell along the wearer's side, were designed to ensure the performers could move easily. For a robotic character with an Industrial Revolution feel created for *La Vie Aménagée*, the funnel-shaped skirt only appeared rigid. A hoop at the base of the skirt provided support, and the surface was flexible foam covered with metallic fabric. The pipe-like arms of the costume look constraining, but the hands were just hidden, monk like, in the wrist openings of the opposite sleeves, which enabled the actress to use her hands when she was out of the audience's view.

Germain always adjusts his costumes to suit the best needs of the production, and of the performers. "I think if someone is ill at ease in their costume, they will not give as good a performance." He recalls a production of *Il Tito* at Opéra National du Rhin. To reflect the opera's Roman setting, he designed a grand warrior costume for the title character. Atypically, he had to design the costume prior to meeting the performer, who joined the production quite late in the rehearsal process. When the singer arrived, "he was nice looking, but very effeminate and very thin. He said to me 'If I wear something like this, the audience will erupt in laughter.'" Germain agreed that the cuirass and greaves would not suit him, and instead created a royal and commanding look with voluminous red robes, edged with gold scrollwork. The costume shop was able to produce the new costume on a quick turnaround. Costumes cannot stand alone, nor should they, Germain explains. "When a production works well, you don't say, 'Oh the costumes were beautiful'; 'Oh the scenery was beautiful.' You say 'Oh what a beautiful production.'"

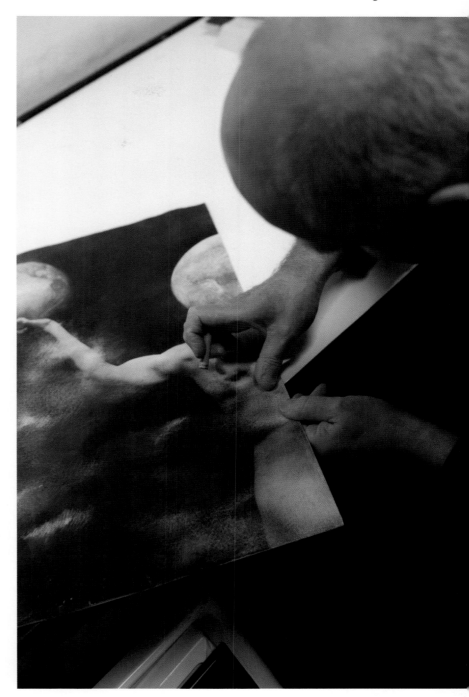

Whether they have created fashions for the stage since childhood, or found the calling later in life, costume designers share a common thread. They routinely balance psychology, sociology, art history, architecture, and accounting. A day's work can run the gamut from riffling through antique photos to calming a self-conscious performer to producing uptown clothes on a downtown budget. Whether creating futuristic armor or picking out the perfect weathered pair of corduroys, costume designers share the goal of finding the best garb for the characters in which to tell their particular story.

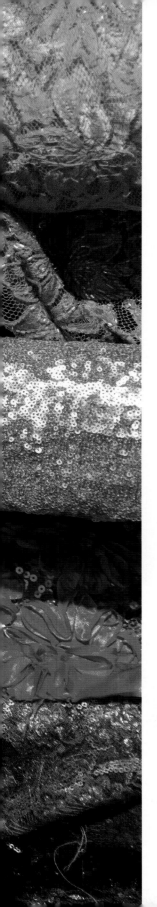

Sourcing Materials

FILLING IN THE OUTLINES

Santo Loquasto's designs for the American Ballet Theatre's *Rodeo* were being rebuilt at Carelli Costumes for a new production. The associate designer had kept careful records of the fabrics used the first time around, but of course they were not necessarily still available several years later. Loquasto used the expected printed calicos for the prairie dresses and western shirts, but in a way that took advantage of the richness and texture of the small prints. The audience would not be able to see the designs on the fabrics, but like brushstrokes in an impressionistic painting they enriched the picture. Monet's green grass is more vibrant because of the touches of yellow, blue, and orange scattered through it. The designer carefully chose a unique grouping of prints for each costume. The skirts for the women used one fabric for the upper skirt, another for the ruffle, and a third for a decorative band just above it. The menswear used different prints for collar, cuffs, yoke, and bandanna. The associate designer went through the book with the shopper, explaining how to choose the different calicos for the effect they created at a distance, not the colors they really contained up close. A yellow fabric scattered with pink and orange daisies did not necessarily need to be replaced with a floral, or even a pink and orange design. Instead, the shopper needed to find a yellow print that cast the same warm glow. The shopper set off across New York's Garment District on her quest. At first, she had to double-check every fabric by laying it out and standing across the room. A green that looked vibrant up close might become murky from a distance if the print was red. The black fabric with pale designs transformed into a mid-tone gray. After a while her eyes and brain adjusted, and she could judge the textiles by squinting at them at arm's length. After several days, she amassed what the associate designer deemed enough choices for a stage full of costumes. The designer made his selections, and the shopper scurried around town buying them before someone else did!

Bright sequins and ribbons embellish fabrics on the walls at Textile Fabrics in Nashville.

Workmen carry rolls of fabric in New York's Garment District.

Sourcing is a crucial aspect of creating costumes. The fabrics and trims serve as the "paint" that colors in the lines of the costume. Choosing the materials is as important a decision for costumes as choosing ingredients is for a chef: without the right flavors and quality, the whole product suffers. Each fabric must not only be the perfect color, but also have the needed print, texture, and stiffness. Before a shopper goes out to find samples, she must also consider logistical questions. Does the costume need to stretch, be washed by machine, or be dyed? Will it have a lining? Will the performer dance, fight, or get wet onstage? Will there be just one dress, or must she buy enough of the fabric for a whole matching chorus?

For a small production, the designer or the assistant designer does the shopping. For larger venues, there is often a separate job of "shopper." While in some parts of the country shopping may be mainly online, in a large city like New York that person makes daily rounds through dozens of stores in the Garment District that sell fabrics, trims, and specialty items like beads, leather, and buttons. Shopping in actual stores is the best way to see accurate color, and to feel the quality and thickness of the fabrics. However, the designer can't just go on a shopping spree. Numerous samples, or "swatches," must be collected before anything can be purchased. The designer needs to see everything together in order to figure out which fabrics

View through a sidewalk display in New York's Garment District.

and trims work best in combination. The designer also must plot out the different outfits each character wears over the course of the play, picking the shade of green or the rough peasant textures that will best enhance the meaning of the scene. And, they must balance all the fabrics that will share the stage, making sure the colors and patterns for the show work well as a whole, imagining the entire picture. Sometimes the designers finish painting their sketches, and then look for fabrics to fulfill their vision. Other times swatching happens earlier in the process—a certain bold stripe or iridescent velvet can inspire the designer's take on a character.

A costume may be made from just one or two fabrics, or from dozens. A large production with hundreds of costumes needs several shoppers to source options for all of the pieces. They often divide by genre so no one person has to hold quite so much information in her head—perhaps one shops the men's fabrics, one the women's, and a third buys all of the nonbuilt pieces like ties, socks, and jewelry. The shoppers organize the swatches, often onto metal rings. Each ring might hold a set of options for a particular character, or the fabrics might be grouped by function: shirtings, tie fabrics, linings. The sheer number of decisions a designer must make can be over-

Customer perusing wares on display at Daytona Trimmings.

whelming. Working sketch by sketch, the designer riffles through the swatches, and picks the main fabrics, accents, linings, trimmings, and buttons. The assistant or shopper helps to track the components needed for each costume, and makes sure that everything has been chosen. Even two fabrics that are nominally the same present dif-ferent variables. When selecting between several heavy red satins, a designer has to weigh the merits of different kinds of shine, whether the fabric falls in rounded or angular folds, and the exact shade of red. At the end of a long meeting, sometimes the weary designer's answer to the offered choices is "what do you think?"

Customer Ivan Horvath and his daughter Eva Miles Horvath select the perfect fringe at M&J Trimmings in New York.

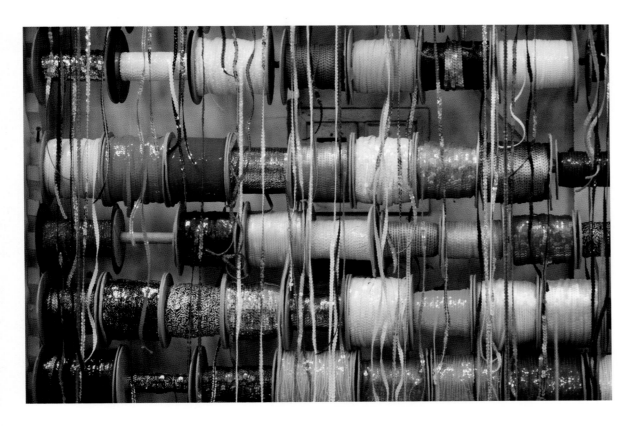

Above and opposite: Employee Chittaranjan Biswas measures red silk at Butterfly Fabrics in New York.

SUPPORTING THE DESIGN—
SHOPPER SARAH BAHR

Assistant designer Sarah Bahr stands at a table piled with sketches, fabric samples, and boxes of shoes paging through an enormous three-ring binder. She pores over the dressing lists and updates the page for the performer who just had a fitting. The show is nearly ready for dress rehearsal, and she is checking her records to ensure that each tie, belt, and pair of earrings has been chosen, approved, labeled, and readied for transfer to the backstage wardrobe crew. She

has organized the spare stash of accessories according to character type so the designer can easily select pieces to fill gaps the next time he meets with her.

Sarah Bahr is an MFA candidate in costume design at the University of Minnesota. Fashion caught her eye from an early age. "My mom is a quilter. I was more interested in clothes," she recalls. She started college in her native Minnesota planning to pursue fashion, but tried some theater courses and was immediately drawn to the collaborative aspect of stage costumes. After college, she came to New York

Embroidered and beaded silks on display at Butterfly Fabrics.

to pursue theater, taking work as a stitcher, but eventually detoured into fine art, and successfully pursued an MA in studio art at NYU. "I did a lot of fiber art in New York and got away from designing theater and really missed this collaborative art form." She returned to Minnesota to be closer to her family, and worked as an assistant designer in Minneapolis at the renowned Guthrie Theater and the Minnesota Opera. She felt at home not only being in the Twin Cities, but also being back in the world of theater design. She decided to pursue a Master's Degree to hone her skills and propel her to the next phase of her career, and possibly into teaching.

In New York Bahr also worked as a shopper. In addition to developing a discerning eye for different kinds of fabrics, she learned that a lot of the job was planning and logistics. She found that sampling a fabric that the designer liked was no help if the store no longer carried it when she returned to buy it. She also learned that shoppers must establish a relationship with stores, and that the etiquette is to always work with the same salesperson. Bahr adds, "Even on a day I might not be buying anything I stopped in to say hello and do some swatching." Cultivating relationships is crucial for a shopper. She might need a fabric put on hold if it is under consideration but not yet ready to buy. And, seasoned salespeople can add valuable suggestions—knowing offhand if the store carries a specific fabric, suggesting alternate fabric types, or checking if they can order larger quantities or an out of stock fabric. A shopper's job is also about endurance—the New York Garment District is a small area, so the most practical mode of transport for shoppers is on foot, stopping back at the costume shop or office once or twice a day. Bahr worked a stint shopping for Santa Fe Opera. "What was fantastic about working for Santa Fe was we shipped all the fabric [directly from the stores], so you didn't have to lug it around New York. I was a little spoiled."

Bahr also learned how to collaborate with a designer. She found it was important to "over swatch," bringing fifteen choices rather than three for a given garment. A full range of choices makes a designer feel confident that they have been given the best options. The shopper should let the designer make the decisions, rather than trying to make them on his or her behalf. However, the shopper should also trust her own sense of artistry. She "learned to trust your gut—[telling herself] yes, this is what they are asking for but maybe this could work too." A designer can't know exactly what will or will not be in stores, so if a shopper sees a stripe in the perfect color and texture, even though they were supposed to look for a paisley, it's worth seeing if the designer might prefer it. Shoppers are usually aspiring designers, and the position is a good stepping-stone to assistant designer jobs. Working as a shopper provides an opportunity to meet designers and impress them with a keen artistic eye and good problem-solving skills.

Sourcing is about more than just fabrics and trims. Bahr's current summer job is as assistant costume designer for *Carmen* at the Santa Fe Opera. When she arrived in Santa Fe, designer Jorge Jara had finished the designs long ago, and the main clothing items were already procured or being constructed. Jara had saved plenty of work for Bahr, however—he put his assistant in charge of accessorizing. For Jara's design, with an aesthetic of eclectic mixes, finding the right details is a big job. She began by going through the opera's stock, pulling out hats, belts, shoes, and jewelry. To fill out the options for Jara to pick from, she also went on lots of shopping excursions. Since the production is set in the mid-twentieth century in the American Southwest, Bahr and Jara were able to shop for what they needed locally. "We went to the Tesuque market to purchase those details that make it a little Southwest, mixed with vintage. We bought a lot of jewelry and turquoise pendants that we made into bolo ties and cowboy hats and boots that are vintage and used so they look really great." Once they had assembled all of the options, Bahr helped Jara accessorize each character and member of the chorus to have a unique style. As they went through the characters' outfits, some custom-built and some assembled from vintage clothing, "my job was quickly finding a belt or earrings that would match, or not match, in a perfect way to create the look." Once Bahr picked up Jara's aesthetic, she assembled the looks herself and the designer just weighed in on the finished product.

Assistant Designer Caitlin Rain surrounded by accessories she must catalog for *Fidelio* at the Santa Fe Opera.

Employee Jackie Lee prepares hanging samples for display at B&J Fabrics in New York.

Employee Anthony Lilly at B&J folds filmy white chiffon.

Lee returns a roll of fabric to the shelf. The paper protects the silk.

A LIBRARY OF TEXTILES—EDUARDO MADRID AT B&J FABRICS

For a shopper trying to use her time wisely, one important strategy is to choose the right store for the project. Some fabric stores stock menswear staples, selling fine wool suitings, rayon bemberg linings, and striped cottons for shirts. Others feature lace or stretch fabrics. For a low-budget production, a shopper will stick to the cheaper stores except for the occasional splurge. For a higher-end production, quality is more important, and fabrics that will last for months or even years of hard use are worth the extra money. For a show expecting a long run, or a drawn-out design process with a long lag time between the swatching and the choosing, a store with a consistent inventory is vital. However, sometimes a unique, quirky find is the priority, and worth the gamble of shopping in stores with rotating stock, even if the desired piece might be sold out by tomorrow.

Often the best places to begin a day of shopping are the stores with a wide range of well-chosen inventory. If a designer had to pick one store from which to procure their whole show, B&J Fabrics in New York would be a likely choice. One of the people responsible for the always-interesting selection is Eduardo Madrid, who is a manager and fabric buyer at the family-owned store. He began as a salesperson twenty-eight years ago, and worked his way up. Since he came from a family of tailors and seamstresses, he had some basic knowledge of the business, but the majority of his training happened at the store. B&J stocks the gamut from retro cotton prints to double-faced knits to iridescent silk chiffons and metallic brocades. "It's like a library. There are so many different things, so many qualities and textures. It was amazing. Basically I learned everything here." A young shopper would agree—when asked by a designer for a type of fabric they have never heard of, rather than confessing ignorance, they head to B&J first. There the salespeople will not only know what it is, they will also be able to present a sample. The best way to understand a textile's properties is by touch, so this is far superior to a quick Internet search.

Once Madrid had mastered the "library," he began to keep up with the fabrics he saw in fashion magazines, suggesting styles for the store to stock. And, if customers repeatedly requested varieties B&J did not have, he took note. Madrid eventually moved up to a manager position, and also became a buyer for the store. He now travels yearly to Paris to the Première Vision fabric show. However, most of the store's buying happens when wholesale vendors come to New York to show their goods, and Madrid and owner Scott Cohen make the selections together. Since costume designers make up a large portion of the store's business, Madrid evaluates potential stock by imagining who might use it, and for what. "When I buy something I have in mind two customers: theater and regular designers." He sees the spectrum of uses one fabric might have, from contemporary fashion to period and specialty looks.

Costume shoppers and fabric stores have a symbiotic relationship. Neophytes in the costume business rely on the expertise of salespeople to guide them through the dizzying array of selections. While everything in the store is labeled and organized, a shopper needs to understand the terminology, and why they might pick one quality over another. Madrid feels that many fresh graduates don't know "what they are looking for or how to differentiate it." They are shaky on the difference between chiffon and charmeuse, or how to tell polyester from silk by touch. Established customers like to be able to come in and see the latest trends, ask the store to hold fabrics, or place special orders. Or, they may just sit for a moment and have a cup of coffee in a calm environment. The store, in return for giving out dozens of free swatches, gets steady business. When a show becomes a hit, costume shops need to buy the same fabrics again and again to make costumes for understudies, replacements, and tours. Long-running shows like *Phantom of the Opera* or *Wicked* prefer to keep buying the designers' original selections, and so the stores will even contact the manufacturers to keep the fabrics from being phased out.

B&J Fabrics caters to costume designers, and also to custom designers for fashion, weddings, and interiors, as well as "regular" customers. Whereas many of the other clients come in to browse, Madrid understands that "costume designers normally know what they want. The regular customers, they bring a picture, they want something for a wedding. They need more guidance. Costume designers have their minds set to the period, what the costume needs to look like." However, he also enjoys making suggestions when they can't find exactly what they envisioned or when they are searching for inspiration. He has several costume design clients who like to come to the store themselves, rather than using shoppers, so they can see whole pieces of fabric and get their creative juices flowing. Designer Anita Yavich is one frequent client who brings her sketches to the store. She has Madrid pull out fabrics he thinks she might use. He piles bolts of fabric on one of the large tables, where she can drape and layer them as she thinks. Madrid is always proud "when I go to the opera and I can see the costume and say 'oh my god I helped with that!' I see it onstage and it's amazing . . . when you see the final product." He frequently recognizes his recommendations on television and film as well. "I love what I do, I love to work with fabrics—this is my life. It's a blessing."

Young shopper Lauren Glenn at Textile Fabrics in Nashville.

Customer Olga Lochbihler checking a bolt of fabric at Textile Fabrics.

Employee Marla Love helps a customer at Textile Fabrics.

Purchasing Manager Tim Blacker in his office at Barbara Matera Ltd. Costume Shop.

SUPPLYING THE CHOICES—
PURCHASING MANAGER TIM BLACKER

At a large costume shop like Barbara Matera Ltd. in New York City, which creates costumes for Broadway, ballets, operas, and occasionally film, a purchasing manager like Tim Blacker oversees several shoppers, and coordinates with the designers. He ensures that all necessary materials for each costume are sampled, chosen, and bought. The city's variety, quality, and reasonable prices mean that even designers from other garment centers like London, Paris, or Los Angeles often prefer to shop the fabrics for their productions in New York.

Blacker has been in his current job for nearly twenty years. He had an early love of the theater, and started out wanting to be an actor, but in college his interest turned to costumes. He studied both fashion and theater, and then went to graduate school in costume design at the University of Illinois. He originally planned to pursue the standard career path, working his way up to designer. "Usually the entry level position is shopper, and then hopefully you get to assist the designer, and then once you assist them for x amount of years, then maybe when they have an excess amount of opportunities being offered at one time and they might throw one over at you. That's the ideal situation, but it doesn't always work that way." After

A selection of fabric samples for the projects Blacker is currently juggling.

some years as an assistant costume designer, rather than wait for an employer to offer him a step up, he opted to leave the rat race for his current position as Purchasing Manager.

"I still have a lot of input . . . I am fulfilled creatively" in this job. When he talks through a show with a designer, discussing fabric ideas for each sketch, he likes to offer up his expertise. "We have designers who have varying degrees of knowledge about fabric, what you can do with it, techniques like embroidery or different processes, and sometimes people never even thought about hand-painting a fabric, or digitally printing, or maybe we could do a creative pleating process on it." He recalls an experience with "a designer who is kind of famous now" at the early end of her career, with a show full of dark dresses. For the first in the pile she said, "I think this is a black fabric, maybe a satin." As they discussed each sketch in turn "they were all mostly black, and she thought they were all mostly satin" so Blacker had his shoppers swatch not only satins, but also crepe, charmeuse, georgette, and lots of other textures. The designer appreciated the effort, and felt comfortable collaborating on fabric choices. "I am just trying to make *their* designs as fabulous as they can be," says Blacker.

Blacker does understand that the fabric used in a costume is ultimately the designer's choice. If a designer selects a piece that looks beautiful but Blacker is afraid it won't hold up to wear and tear, he can suggest something else more practical, but they might not agree. These situations make him cringe. He pictures two months hence, knowing "our shop's label is in it, and the wardrobe crew is sitting backstage mending it for the hundredth time." Once a show is up and running, replacements for worn-out costumes or new cast members are ordered by the producers directly from the shop that built the original. While the shop keeps detailed records of which fabrics were used and where they were purchased, often the same fabrics are no longer available. He recalled a recent rebuild for an understudy for an ice show. The shop swatched alternate fabrics and "I called the designer . . . and she was grateful that I involved her in it, even two years after the fact." The designer appreciated the chance to preserve creative control over her design, even if it might have been faster and easier for the shop not to consult her. "I said we can make the decision for you—but it's not really our job."

Customer Beverly Barton at Textile Fabrics.

A customer selects the perfect tweed.

Filling in the outlines of the costume by sourcing the gabardines, ribbons, and buttons is a vital artistic step. Each item is a piece of the puzzle. Fantastic, sheer cutwork velvet in vivid teal will only be a brilliant find if the right lining supports it. It needs to be backed with a fabric that has the exact same drape as the velvet so the two can move in unison. Shoppers help designers to combine materials artfully. They find a delicate trimming to edge a busy print, or crystal buttons to liven up a modest tweed jacket. While shoppers want to find the perfect choice for each ingredient in a costume, the most important aspect is not the separate parts, nor how the items look up close, but the total effect they create onstage.

3

Draping and Cutting

SCULPTING THE SHAPE

The actors took their curtain call, marking the end of the dress rehearsal. From the back of the Pearl Theatre, the draper breathed a sigh of relief—the designer (the author) was happy, the leading ladies were happy, and the director seemed preoccupied with the lighting. She could declare these costumes done and move on to her next project. The overall look of this Off Broadway production was simple and elegant, much more so than the construction process had been. For this version of the classical tragedy *Andromache*, the title character wore a loose underdress pulled in by a corset-like bodice, giving her the more "foreign" look called for by the storyline. The other leading lady, Hermione, had an elegant empire-waisted gown, a modernized take on ancient Greek drapery. Although Andromache's corseted look appeared more complex, Hermione's dress had actually been the greater challenge for the draper. Shaping the upper edge of the corset to sit just below the bust line took some finesse, but fitting a shape tightly to an actress' curves is relatively simple—it's either right or it's wrong. Sculpting Hermione's dress so that the fabric would fall in fluttery waves without hiding the actress' body like a tent had been an ordeal. At the draper's suggestion, the designer had already made a change from the initial sketch prior to the fitting, reducing the volume of the skirts to lie flatter over the stomach.

Above and opposite: Costumer Quitterie Lassallette and intern Edith DeBeco trace patterns and cut hound's-tooth stretch fabric for a set of jackets for a commercial event.

However, when the actress had her first fitting, her face fell. She had seen Andromache's flattering costume and felt like she was coming in a very distant second. Since the two characters vie for the king's attentions, the designer was willing to adjust the design further to ensure that both the actress and her character felt attractive enough. The draper tried different sizes and angles of pleats to create a slightly lower neckline and more shaping for the bust while preserving the appearance of natural, graceful folds. She reworked the over-drape following the new design so it was more like a cape and less like sleeves, and framed the actress' slim arms rather than covering them. At the second fitting the actress was clearly happier, and free to focus her energies on conveying her character's downward spiral of unrequited love.

The draper (sometimes also called the cutter) is the person responsible for giving shape to the designer's sketches—translating them into a pattern and then overseeing the process of producing the actual costume. The draper and designer talk through the designs, discussing a long list of aesthetic and practical concerns: how both the actor and the costume itself need to be able to move; where the costume will fasten; what sorts of fabrics will be used; what support structures or special undergarments are needed; and any other unusual features. If the show is set in an historical time period, an experienced draper will already know the shapes the pattern pieces should follow. However, they will still refer to the designer's research to be sure to reproduce the lines, proportions, and details that most inspired these particular costume designs.

Drapers help adjust the performers' bodies to suit their characters, figuring out a way to hide a baby bump or broaden a slender tough guy. These artisans also serve as engineers, finessing a slinky, fitted sheath dress so that it hugs every curve of the leading lady without ever riding up, or balancing a tall, structured collar for the villain so it curves like a barricade behind his head. They sculpt capes that look carelessly flung over the shoulder, but whose folds cascade elegantly down the wearer's back in the same configuration every time. Tailors craft trousers that look like regular suit pants, but allow the wearer to do a full split without fearing a wardrobe malfunction.

The first step is to create the pattern. If using the draping method, they pad the dress form to the dimensions of the performer's body in order to have an accurate base on which to work. They use fabric to sculpt the shape on the form, pin it in place, and then transfer the information to paper. A cutter or a tailor creates the pattern two-dimensionally by drafting a pattern onto paper using rulers, formulas, and an experienced eye to convert body measurements into clothing shapes. Theatrical patterns are created for a specific individual, rather than in generic sizes like store-bought clothing. If the performer will wear a corset, hoopskirt, or hunchback, pattern makers have to take that into account as well.

Whichever way the template is created, the next step is a mock-up: a rough draft of the costume usually built in muslin fabric. When a performer tries on the mock-up, the designer and draper together evaluate whether the shape is working aesthetically, and also if the actor can move and breathe with comfort. Each costume and each body are different, so this mock-up step is worth the time to be sure the real fabric is not wasted. They customize each garment so the fit is flattering to the actor (or unflattering, if the character is supposed to look unkempt). No matter how experienced a designer is, they often change their mind about details once they see the three-dimensional shape.

Drapers supervise the team who will cut out and sew the mock-up and the finished costume. Most drapers and cutters (strangely given the job title) do not cut out the fabric themselves. They work with an assistant, usually called a first hand, who cuts out the fabric pieces, and then passes the project to the stitchers, who construct the garment. A small costume shop has one or two teams, a larger shop many more. Some shops have separate pattern makers in charge of men's wear and women's wear—those in charge of the menswear are usually called tailors.

Tailor Valentina Abramova tracing patterns onto muslin at Barbara Matera Ltd.

Costumer Lisa Coppolani at Atelier Caraco Canezou in Paris cuts out paper patterns.

Coppolani and fellow costumer Celia Guillet create couture at Atelier Caraco.

COSTUME ARCHITECT—
KJERSTEN LESTER-MORATZKA

Draper Kjersten Lester-Moratzka puts the dress on the mannequin and surveys the silhouette of the frothy orange skirt, seeing if the myriad of ruffles and stiffeners beneath are finally forming the belled shape she wants. She pats and fluffs the fabric, then gives the dress a twirl to see if the volume remains constant. Some of the lower layers still seem a little limp, so she has her assistant cut some more strips of sheer sunshine-colored organza. These will be gathered into yet more ruffles, and added in tiers to bolster the bottom sections. She turns her attention to the sleek black bodice, checking that the fasteners leave no gaps in the back.

Lester-Moratzka has been Principal Women's Draper at the Santa Fe Opera for many years. During the summers she works professionally, but she spends the rest of the year teaching her skills to some of the nation's top costume production students. She taught at Ohio University for many years, but recently returned to her alma mater and joined the faculty at the North Carolina School of the Arts. "I wanted to be an architect but it takes so long to make a building, to see if your ideas work. I wanted faster gratification," she explains. Lester-Moratzka enrolled in college as a history major with a minor in art. Having decided against studying architecture, but unsure what to pursue instead, she took a semester off, and found herself with an internship at the Children's Theater of Minneapolis. She had never felt any pull toward theater, but she knew how to sew and needed a way to fill her time. Despite her inexperience, she was assigned as the assistant for legendary designer Desmond Heeley since no one on the staff was available. In this case her naiveté served her well, because she wasn't distracted from her work by being starstruck or intimidated by Heeley's fame. In fact, they got along quite well, and "he's the one that told me 'you know darling, you can go to graduate school and do this for a living.'" She applied to the North Carolina School of the Arts on Heeley's recommendation. At the time such Master's programs specifically in costume production were quite rare in the U.S. Recently they have become more prevalent. "I am part of that first generation, and we are the generation that is now teaching."

Draper Kjersten Lester-Moratzka working on a dress for the title character in *Carmen* at the Santa Fe Opera.

A stitcher binds the edge of Carmen's hem.

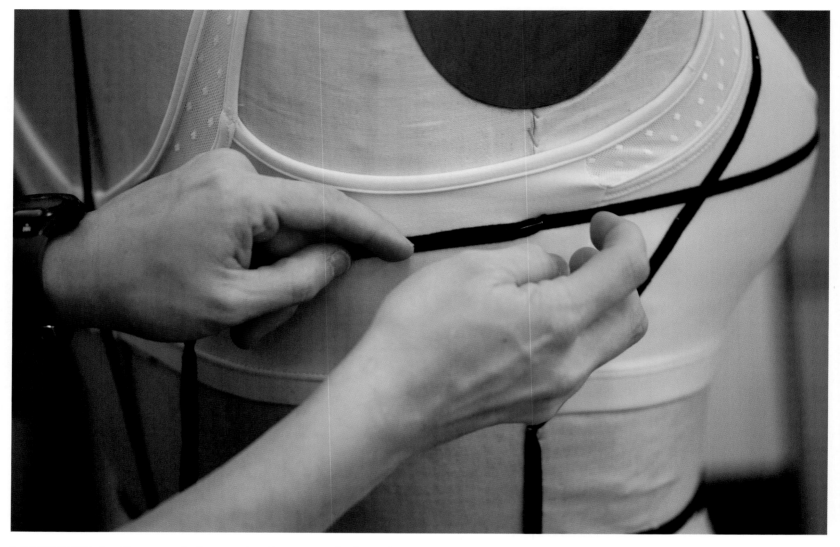

A draper uses ribbon to outline a garment's shape on a dress form as preparation for creating a pattern by the draping method.

Lester-Moratzka is known for beautifully fitting garments, for her flexibility, and her ability to keep up with a challenge, all of which make her an ideal candidate to dress leading ladies of the opera. Solving the puzzle of opera designers' fantastical creations fulfills her original urge to design buildings. "The engineering part [of draping] feeds the part of my brain that wanted to be an architect—looking at something and seeing not just the outside but what is going on on the inside." Certainly, she has frequent chances to test her ideas and see if they work.

One of her first big projects at the Santa Fe Opera was for French designer Laurent Pelly, for *La Traviata*. Pelly needed the draper's help reconciling the vision in his head with what he was able to draw, and his limited English compounded the challenge. The designer gave Lester-Moratzka three different sketches of "this giant pink thing. They were all in the same flavor but not the same dress," plus a large assortment of pink fabrics. When the designer brought her a picture of a peony flower it provided the crucial piece of information to make the vision come together. "I said ok, sure . . . we can turn a peony into a dress. I'll get right on that!" she chuckles. In addition to the three sketches, Pelly gave her a packet of research from 1950s fashion. "He had lots of pictures of edge finishes and treatments and rows and rows of ruffles and layers and whatnot, so it [made clear it] wasn't petals he wanted, it was the idea of the volume [of the peony]."

The dress they created had a simple, fitted strapless bodice, but an extremely elaborate skirt, with layers of fabric in slightly different lengths and textures. "It ended up using something insane like 121 yards of five zillion different shades of pink." In addition to capturing the volume and silhouette of a peony, Pelly threw a train at the back, and the skirt's layers folding back on themselves at the front into the mix. The leading lady, Natalie Dessay, was quite agile, and the director wanted her to be able to run up and down the stairs. Lester-Moratzka strove to find a way to keep all the frothy layers open in the front, to help the singer maneuver. "We actually did fittings on the back deck of the theater—she would be running up and down the back steps to see if it was working. It was a really great collaborative effort between Laurent and Natalie and myself trying to figure out what this dress was."

Lester-Moratzka had another chance to use her architectural brain when the Santa Fe Opera did *Tales of Hoffman*. The opera contains three separate stories, each featuring one of Hoffman's past loves. Usually different singers play the three women, but for this production the director chose to cast one singer as all three. To emphasize the theatrical style of the production, the singer changed costumes onstage between roles. For any show set before 1900, noticeable zippers are not an option, as that mechanism did not yet exist, and Velcro is not only ugly, but also noisy. The first dress, which was put on in the dressing room, used a standard theater trick. It appeared to be laced up the back like a corset, an attractive fastening that is usually quite slow to undo, but instead of having one string zigzag across the opening, looping through both sets of holes, each side has

its own string. Both strings get looped around a thin rod of metal at the center. Tension holds it all in place, but when the rod is pulled out from the top, the dress falls open, revealing the singer in a corset and bloomers.

The difficulty was making the next gown in such a way that other performers could dress the singer and secure the costume with just one fastener. "It was this enormous ball gown kind of a thing and it was this huge confection of five million layers of ruffles, and rows and rows of trim, but the whole thing had to go on onstage. It was on a display mannequin onstage and two supers [supernumeraries, nonsinging actors] had to take it off the mannequin and she just raised her hands above her head and they slid it on." To support the weight of the gown, Lester-Moratzka used bustle-like cages of steel on the inside of the dress, one resting on each hip. These structures, resembling a covered wagon turned on end, held the skirts away from the body and left the singer room to move her legs. The bodice, stiffened with lots of metal boning, had a low V neckline in the back, and the opening butted neatly when a large, sturdy backpack buckle clicked shut. Since the dress was so heavy, the singer would only be able to walk naturally if the weight balanced perfectly. The draper distributed the weight as evenly as she could with the dress on a mannequin. But she could only gauge her efforts by testing it in motion. So, being the right size, she put the dress on and walked around the costume shop. Her assistant stood ready with counterweights and pinned them in place when the dress listed to the back. By the time the singer came in for her final fitting, the dress balanced well, and needed only very subtle adjustments.

Draper Robert Manning patterns additions to a suit of superhero armor for a Broadway musical at Parsons-Meares, Ltd.

Draper Janet Parran and stitcher Margarita Romero make some final adjustments to a highly structured skirt for *Shrek the Musical* at Barbara Matera Ltd.

Draper Annick LeSuperbe at Mine Barral Verges in Paris cuts out a garment.

LeSuperbe explains the next construction step to intern Clara Signoud.

TRANSFORMING BODIES—TRIFFIN MORRIS

Triffin Morris' specialty is offbeat costumes and unusual problem solving. For the title green ogre in *Shrek, the Musical*, Morris created a monstrous body for leading man Brian Darcy James, who, as she explains, was "soaking wet 150 lbs. or something like that and he's got to be a 300 pound guy." The trick is that foam tends to look like padding, and not real body fat, which has weight to it. But clearly the designer Tim Hatley did not want James to have to act the show with too much extra ballast weighing him down. Instead, the costumers had to find a balance between using foam to create much of the bulk, and then "fatty looking stuff" in a layer on top. For the fat

layer, they experimented to find a good balance between lighter and heavier particles. "Micro beads themselves are sort of fluffy and the plastic beads were too heavy so the combination is key . . . there's actually measuring cups involved to get the perfect formula . . . and there's a funnel. So that's new," the draper explains, laughing.

Morris is frequently called upon to make body padding. "I feel like I'm doing my job right when I walk into the fitting . . . a fat pad or even just a dress, and the actor puts it on and you can see them start to become that person." Customizing the body shape to each performer and each character intrigues her. "If you look at real people, you will soon discover that you will find any shape and

Draper Bineke Fokkens-Kiernan works on an undergarment for *Carmen* at the Santa Fe Opera.

size . . . and there aren't that many pictures available of real, heavy people, naked. You end up on strange websites," she says matter-of-factly. After a conversation with the designer, she roughs out a draft in foam on a dress form. She focuses on where the person carries their weight and the sculptural form of the body being created. She makes sure to discuss logistical as well as aesthetic concerns with the designer. When creating a full body fat suit for a production of *Model Apartment*, Morris and designer Jenny Mannis collaborated with the actress, Diane Davis, to find the best functionality for an onstage sex scene. They worked through which clothes would come off during the scene, and put in fastenings to attach others directly to the padding, to ensure the false body would not show.

A draping challenge that happens more often than one might think is making clothing come off "magically" onstage. Morris created a skirt that remained standing by itself after the owner walked away for the musical *Nine*. For the Broadway show *All Shook Up*, she engineered a drab ensemble that flew off to reveal a new colorful outfit underneath. The actress had to stand still in a doorway, arms out, and the clothes came off with one quick pull by a stagehand far off-stage who, as Morris dead-pans, "does not know from clothes." The garment had to split strategically not only at the front but also along the arms. Morris found the right combinations of snaps and other closures to secure it just enough to hold until the magic moment. And, the wires had to be attached at strategic places so the tug would

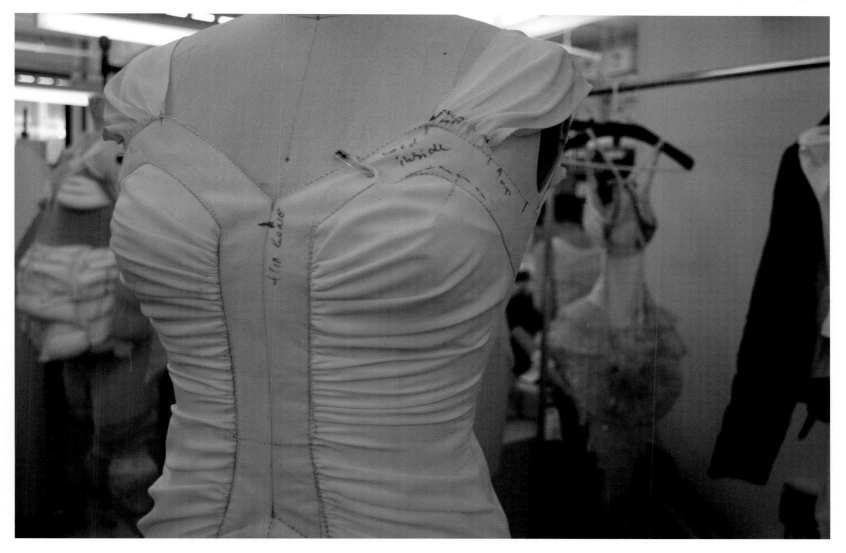

A mock-up of a dress for *Memphis the Musical* awaits adjustments after a fitting at Tricorne costume shop in New York.

open the snaps and pull the clothes, rather than either ripping the fabric or yanking the actress backwards. Her job was made possible thanks to good planning by designer David C. Woolard, who created a "friendly" design. "In the places where he thought I would need to put closures, he put a seam, so I wasn't having to make anything up." She recalls that at the first fitting Woolard "was dubious of my solution . . . he said 'Really, it's going to work like that?' But it did. That was fun"

For Morris, working in costume technology is what she was born to do. "I feel like fabric is my medium . . . Any time I've sat down to paint or draw, I couldn't produce the image in my head on the paper. But I can do that with fabric. I can imagine what it looks like

and I can make it come out that way." Morris' father first introduced her to theater. He directed shows and taught, and since she loved to sew she was often drafted to help out with costumes. However, the passion did not strike her until several years after college, when on a whim she helped out sewing at a local theater in Milwaukee. By chance, the theater housed a well-known school called the Professional Theatre Training Program, and soon she found herself pursuing an MFA degree. For an internship to round out her studies, she went to New York to work as a first hand. She received several offers from shops, but chose to work at Euroco because "I had heard that [co-owner and draper] Werner Kulovits . . . was a mad genius and I thought: I want to know what a mad genius is. And once I had

Tailor Jerome Schram assembling pieces of a fantastical robe for *Le Rossignol* at the Santa Fe Opera.

Schram marking fabric with tailor's chalk.

started . . . I never wanted to do anything else." After a few years in the industry, Morris worked her way up to draper.

Draping a large number of garments for *Wicked* is one of Morris' proudest achievements. "Susan Hilferty's design work on that was groundbreaking, I think. [Hilferty won a Tony Award for her costumes.] It's challenging, it's interesting. . . When I see the show there is always something I did onstage." Morris was newly hired at Tricorne costume shop when they started work on the show, so she was not caught up in ongoing projects and thus was available to take on a large percentage of the patterning. The costume shapes were very complicated to figure out, for both designer and draper. Since most of the clothes were asymmetrical, Hilferty drew all four sides of the costumes in her designs. But even so, some questions could only be resolved in 3-D, after Morris began draping. Seams and shapes were hard to track and connect as they wound their way around the body. For a long-running juggernaut like *Wicked*, with multiple touring companies, costume shops make many versions of the garments. Morris enjoys that challenge too. "Even if it's the same costume, it's for a different person. I feel like there is always something to learn. There is a way to make it better—prettier, cleaner, a smoother line. I feel like you've done it right when you step back and say 'I can't imagine that as a bolt of fabric. It looks like it was always that dress.'"

TRANSLATING THE SKETCH—DAVID AREVALO

David Arevalo and his team cluster around a maroon turn of the century dress to be featured in the premiere of the opera *Dr. Sun Yat-sen* at the Santa Fe Opera. Having resolved the fit and shape of the luminous silk and wool dress, he needed to figure out how to turn paisley cutwork-lace fabric into a facsimile of custom embroidery. His team of stitchers cut the motifs carefully into a variety of clusters. Arevalo pins them in different combinations along the hem, bodice, and sleeve, trying to capture the flavor of the scrolls and flourishes in the designer's sketch. Once the designer, James Schuette, approves the attempt, Arevalo will complete the layout, and the stitchers will spend many hours carefully securing the pieces by hand.

A very different challenge for *Dr. Sun Yat-sen* has been prioritizing the resources to decorate a traditional Chinese tunic. When Arevalo did the first calculation of how much trim would be required to reproduce the designer's sketch, it needed $600 worth, more than was budgeted. The designer preferred to use the chosen trim, which was $10 per yard, rather than something cheaper. Instead, Arevalo had to find a way to keep the look, but without replicating every line in the designer's sketch. "I had some license to scale it back but still try to give the designer what he's asking for. You can't just start taking it away everywhere, so it was a real process—I needed a way to use less but do it carefully so it doesn't look sad."

In eight seasons at the Santa Fe Opera, David Arevalo worked his way up from apprentice to draper. This is his first full season at that rank. Previously he spent the summer as a draper's assistant and before that as a first hand. During the year he is a staff cutter/draper at the well-known arts school, University of Cincinnati College of Music, making costumes for the opera and drama departments. As an assistant draper last season, Arevalo was in charge of some of his own projects, including a fantastical jack-in-the-box judge robe for a nightmare scene in *Oscar*, an opera about Oscar Wilde. The designer, David C. Woolard, wanted the sleeves to look "sproingy" and collapsible like a real jack-in-the-box. Every ring supporting the sleeve was a different size: the armhole was small, the middle of the sleeve got bigger, and then it decreased again to the wrist. "Every ring had [supporting] hooping—some of the smaller ones were steel hooping, the larger ones were nylon rod so it was more comfortable for the actors. We tried some millinery plastic but it snapped in the fitting, so that was a big experiment and collaboration." Arevalo wanted to capture the precise proportions in Woolard's sketch. Although his first draft was close, the designer requested some of the hoops be a bit larger or smaller. Every accordion fold in the sleeve had to have its own pattern piece, a slightly larger or smaller arc of fabric. Every adjustment to the size of a ring meant redoing the arcs for both adjoining sides. "There was so much math—it was outrageous," Arevalo says, shaking his head ruefully.

Draper David Arevalo with two of his team members, Emma Hankin and Siri Nelson, in the workroom at the Santa Fe Opera.

A dress for the opera *Dr. Sun Yat-sen* ready for a final fitting.

Arevalo's team cuts apart black lace to combine into faux-embroidery.

A draper uses a pounce wheel to trace markings from fabric onto pattern paper.

Drapers balance artistry and physics to translate the designer's vision into a wearable sculpture. They shift modes from bespoke tailoring to athletic stretch wear to glittering gowns. They use their talents to adapt historical shapes to modern bodies and modern choreography. However, whether crafting sleek body-hugging pieces, flowing drapery, or skirts held up by metal struts, the draper's best contribution is to make all these engineering marvels appear onstage to be simply clothing.

4

Fabric Embellishment

CREATING A CUSTOM SURFACE

"What do you thirst for?" was the theme that choreographer Christopher K. Morgan chose to explore for his dance piece for CityDance Ensemble's yearly concert about global warming. It was up to the costume designer (the author) to figure out how the desired dry and dusty feeling could translate to fabric. Costumers commonly use cheesecloth for a gauzy, cobwebby look, but since it doesn't stretch, body-conscious modern dance costumes demanded another method. Stretch mesh fabric struck her as a good substitute: delicate looking, but easily washable and sturdy enough to withstand the company's rigorous international touring schedule. However, beyond a few feet away, the fabric looked smooth and uninteresting. She found other stretch fabrics with more interesting textures, but none of them had the fragile appearance she felt would give the piece the right pathos. Unable to solve her quandary at the drawing board, the designer experimented with samples of the fabric. Printed and painted-on textures just seemed to either look like tie dye or lizard scales. She tried different ways of sewing actual textures—pinches at random intervals and tucks that formed a series of curved ridges. Her pile of scraps caught her eye, and she decided to play with layers. She stacked pieces of the beige fabric, and cut irregularly shaped holes, one layer at a time, cutting a smaller hole in each successive layer. The holes made a pattern like a topographical map, and parts of the costume were now more transparent than others. The choreographer loved how the costumes appeared eroded, and also looked like shifting sands.

Sometimes, no matter how many beautiful and unusual options the stores have, the perfect fabric for a project doesn't exist, so it must be created or adapted. Dyeing is the simplest kind of modification—a fabric has all the right qualities, except for color. Sometimes dye is used to transform a white fabric into a vibrant color, sometimes a too-bright hue is toned down a shade duller. Dyeing is used most often on dancewear and other specialty costumes. These costumes require fabric that will stretch

A worker at Atelier Caraco Canezou in Paris puts finishing touches on a skirt. The rows of lace have been added to a netting background to create a custom striped lace fabric.

Draper Janet Parran and Stitcher Luba Flek at Barbara Matera Ltd. in New York discuss the final construction phase of some custom-printed pants for *The Lion King*.

and move in certain ways, and compromise is not an option. The fabric is selected for its function, and visual aspects are what can be adjusted. If a fabric needs not just a custom color, but also a custom design or pattern, a whole range of painting and printing options are available, depending on budget, time, and quantities needed. Fabrics can be painted freehand, stenciled, batiked, silk-screened, and certain fabrics can also be printed digitally. Painting can add an extra bit of color to a pre-printed fabric, such as turning white dots multicolored, or the artwork can be created from scratch. Painting also adds shading and dimension to forms, such as fake musculature and armor, and it creates dirt and weathering so clothing looks lived-in. Sometimes an all-over pattern is created, like a plaid or wood-grain

texture, and sometimes the design is fit to the shape of the garment and the body, like the famous unitards for *Cats*. The goal of a costume painter is for the work to "read"—meaning that the design has the desired effect from the viewpoint of the audience—whether it is close up in a cabaret, or across an ice rink. Painters, together with the designer, calibrate the scale and boldness to achieve the desired look, be it subtle shading, impressionistic effects, or sharp graphics.

The sewing machine is another tool costumers use to create pattern and texture. Stitchers anchor rows of ribbons onto fabric to make or enhance a stripe or plaid. Or, fabric can be pleated, tucked, quilted, or irregularly scrunched to create all kinds of textures, from elegant sunburst pleats on a chiffon dance skirt to a fabric that appears to

A stitcher at Matera's assembles a garment out of custom-printed fabric.

be tree bark or lizard skin. Stage lighting and distance both tend to flatten out the colors and shapes of a costume, so adding texture and variety to the surface are very important for creating a rich and interesting look onstage. Lace, mesh, and translucent fabrics can be layered to combine colors and patterns. And, of course, all sorts of decoration can be applied to fabric, from the flash of beading, sequins, and metal studs to traditional items like braid, lace, embroidery, and buttons. Embellishment is limited only by imagination (or laundry concerns!). Costumes may be decorated with rubber caulking, metal washers, fiber optics, or Christmas ornaments from the dollar store.

A mid-sized professional costume shop usually has a separate job called painter-dyer while a small shop uses just one person for "crafts" (specialty items like armor, hats, and masks) in addition to paint and dye work. Large markets like New York City have stand-alone businesses specializing in painting and dyeing, and many of the costume shops send their dye work out, rather than having the facilities on-site. However, Parsons-Meares, LTD, which is known for its work on shows like *Cats* and *The Lion King*, employs several full-time painters in-house.

Margaret Peot at Parsons-Meares, Ltd. in New York paints monkey tails for the Broadway musical *Wicked*.

A view of the paint studio at Parson-Meares, Ltd.

LIZARDS AND CATS—PAINTER PARMELEE TOLKAN

Parmelee Tolkan is one of these painters, and she has been painting costumes for close to forty years. A recent project reminded her of her longevity in the business—she painted the lizard costumes for a remount of Edward Albee's famous play *Seascape*, and she also painted the originals thirty years earlier. She was one of the painters who developed the distinctive custom-painted costumes for *Cats*. After it became an international hit, the costume designer, John Napier, took her to Canada, Mexico, and Austria to teach painters there to replicate the look. One of the challenges of *Cats* was to replicate the "liney" hand-drawn aesthetic of the designer's magic marker sketches. Tolkan credits her colleague at the time, Martin Izquierdo, with thinking to use squeeze bottles to achieve the "scratchy painting" effect. "How simple is that?" she laughs. In addition to being skilled with color and a paintbrush, costume painters must figure out which techniques will work best to create a desired effect. Experimentation is an important part of the job, and they use common materials like masking tape in addition to specialized products. Paint may be applied with anything from wood-graining tools to airbrushes to a toothbrush.

For complicated projects like *Cats*, the painters calibrate the design motifs to the individual body. The performer tries on a plain white mock-up unitard first, and while it is stretched to the shape of the body the painter marks waist, knees, elbows, and other landmarks on it in pencil or pen, along with a rough version of the shapes to be painted. Placing the paint motifs can't be easily done from measurements alone, as the fabric stretches different amounts around different parts of the body. The draper then transfers these markings to a paper pattern. Her assistant traces the outline of the pattern pieces, along with the painting guidelines, on the actual fabric for the finished garment. Next, the painter stretches and paints the fabric, and afterwards returns it to the workroom where they will finish the cutting and sewing process.

While studying scenic design at Smith College, Tolkan met renowned costume designer Willa Kim, who was visiting as a guest artist. Kim hired Tolkan to help out on a Broadway production of *Lysistrata*. Her job was shopping for pots and pans and then making armor out of them. As she recalls, "meanwhile over on the side were these two artists, who kept coming in and out with this fabulous painting which was all for [the leading lady's] costumes, and my eyes are going sideways." Kim noticed the young Tolkan's interest, and asked if she would like to help paint textiles. "I just kind of jumped in. I did a sample, and apparently either she was so desperate for the money or the sample was good enough. And then I went on from there, which is the more important part."

Over the years in New York Tolkan sometimes worked in costume shops, and sometimes independently. She currently has her own studio outside the city, but she also works at the Parsons-Meares shop when projects are too large to transport or are on a very tight timetable. She developed her skills through experimentation and practice and by learning from colleagues with different methodologies. She herself started painting as a scenic artist, while colleagues had training in fabric design and dyeing. Tolkan archives samples from past projects, and refers to them when she replicates a costume, or sometimes just to reference a technique. "I think one of the things I've done that I'm proudest of . . . and I know it's a silly thing . . . was that Emperor costume for Disney on Parade. It was double the height of a man, and it had very deep cuffs, and they went all the way down to the ground. They shaded from pale yellow to a really deep red, with a running pattern on them, and I figured out this very complicated stencil. But, I'm not sure if in this day and age, it wouldn't be best done a different way."

During initial meetings with designers at Parsons-Meares, owner Sally Ann Parsons brings in her longtime collaborator Tolkan and asks her opinion on the fabric selections. Depending on the intended paint treatment, only certain fibers like nylon, silk, or wool will give good results. When working with a designer to develop a new costume, the painters do samples of different colors and techniques, often on several kinds of fabric, for the designer to choose from. Even though computers can now do custom designs, Tolkan doesn't think costume painters will be replaced any time soon. Digital printing is not necessarily cheaper for small quantities, and it takes multiple tries to calibrate the color. Also, printing can only be used at the outset of a project, not once a costume has been cut and built.

A painter adds color to an appliqué for the back of a jacket for the Santa Fe Opera's production of *Carmen*.

Peot toning leather platform boots at Parsons-Meares.

Designers give the painters sketches, often accompanied by research, to show them how the costume should look. Tolkan painted a body suit of muscles, as if with no skin, for performer David Byrne, and referred to anatomy books as she worked. "Research is nice, but some of the sketches you get are very painterly and they don't need a lot of other things to tell you how it should look." Tolkan prefers to work on more evocative designs. "I have to say that for me, of all the designers Willa Kim was the most exciting, because she always had such interesting sketches, and the sketches were very painterly. She wanted you to be a painter." On Tolkan's current project, the designer "doesn't want us to be painters, she wants it to look completely mechanical. It needs to be painted to get what her effect is, but she is not interested in seeing [a human touch], so it's all airbrush."

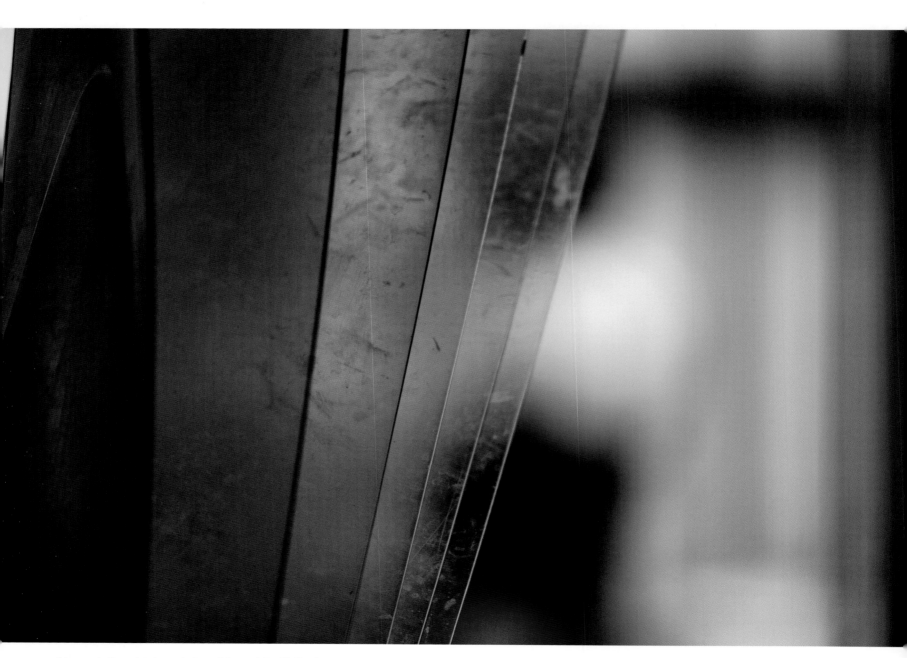

A heavy plastic curtain keeps toxic particles contained in the dye room.

Dyer Iris Litwin mixing dyes at Parsons-Meares, Ltd.

Free-flowing paint used for silk.

FROM TRADITIONAL TO DIGITAL— PAINTER-DYER CAROLINE DIGNES

Caroline Dignes fishes in a pot of dye with tongs, shakes the droplets of teal-colored water from her sample, and then carries it to the sink. Her gloved hands hold the fabric under the faucet until the run-off is clear, and then she clips it up to dry. She examines it critically, comparing the hue to a floral print swatch, checks her notes, and then starts water heating for another attempt. Before the shop can cut and build a glamorous 1940s slip, she must tint the silk the same soft aqua as the sheer flowered dress to be worn over it. She dons her dust mask and mixes a new formula of colored powders, this time adding more blue.

Dignes is a young painter-dyer who works at the Santa Fe Opera during the summers and at Oregon Shakespeare Festival the remainder of the year. "Right now I am still just learning everything I can and I haven't quite figured out where to go with it." She has trained with traditional Asian artisans in remote villages and learned cutting-edge software for textile printers. "I am really fulfilled by the work that I do for theater but I think I'd like to continue to pursue my interest in artisans around the world . . . I'm interested in textile design and fabric design." Dignes, who studied studio art and anthropology in college, traveled to India to study natural dyes. She apprenticed with an artisan who does bandhani, a traditional tie dye technique. "It makes those little tiny circle dots and they are all tied

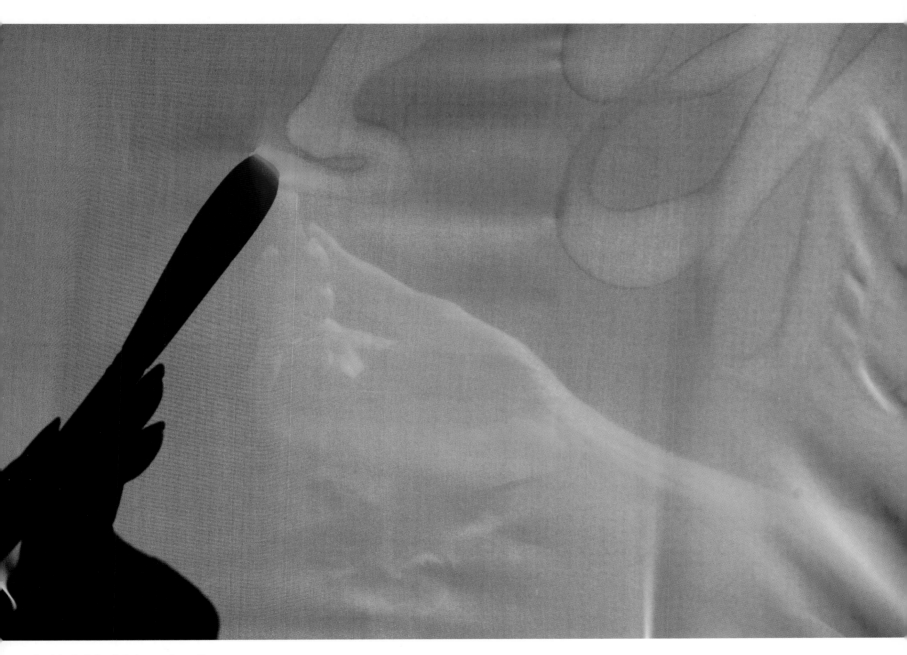

A painter tests brushstrokes on sheer silk.

with your fingernails." She also worked with a group in Laos for six weeks.

At the Oregon Shakespeare Festival, whose costume department is known for intensive textile treatments, Dignes had a chance to learn many unusual techniques. She recalls a production of *Into the Woods* where the designer Linda Roethke envisioned a clear vinyl cape for Cinderella with an elaborate black scrollwork design. Dignes experimented with different types of paints, and the draper tried sewing black trimming in spiral designs, but nothing created the impact the designer desired. Then, Dignes remembered the vinyl cutter in the props shop, which she had previously used to make stencils. The machine cuts out an image created with computer software, and for stenciling she had affixed the sticky vinyl shapes to the fabric while she painted in the holes. But in this case, since the base was already vinyl, the stencil could *be* the design. "The whole thing was completely waterproof. I soaked a sample in water for an hour to check, because this is for the outdoor stage so another concern is that these things are going to get rained on." Once the plan was in place, she created the cape's intricate black design in segments. "I made myself a little map because it was so big I couldn't peel and place it as one giant sticker—I had to break it apart and the map was so I could remember where I was going."

Choosing whether to use digital or traditional printing methods is determined by the look the designer wants, and by logistics. Considerations include the resources of the theater, the yardage needed, and the type of fabric being used. For the cook in the fairytale *Le Rossignol* at Santa Fe Opera, the designer's sketch showed a pattern of repeated ovals around the hem with what Dignes interpreted as "some sort of flower design around." She plans to do a screen print, which works better for multiple repeats. If she were at Oregon Shakespeare Festival it could be a stencil, as she could make a dozen easily with the vinyl cutter, but the opera doesn't have a comparable machine. Sending it out to have the design digitally printed could also have been an option, but the designer chose a fabric incompatible with the process.

For certain projects, digital printing is by far the best solution. Also for *Into the Woods* in Oregon, Cinderella's stepsisters wore dresses that appeared to be made of couture brand shopping bags. The designer would have been happy to cut up real bags and use them, and for a previous show Roethke had done an outfit of garbage bags, but the head of the costume shop vetoed a repeat of that idea immediately. She said, "Our shows run 120 times—they need to last. The plastic bag thing is not cutting it," Dignes recalled. Instead, they had it printed by dye sublimation on shiny polyester satin, a process where heat bonds the color to synthetic fabric. "It had the look of the bags, but it was fabric. Because it was digitally printed it had those crisp lines, and also we needed a lot of yardage. So, digital printing was the only way we could accomplish all we needed." Dignes collaborated with the draper as she created the graphic designs, so that the Versace and Juicy Couture logos would print exactly as needed to recreate the designer's sketches. With the accuracy of the computer, she could modify the logos to be the exact right size and angle for each pattern piece, and they were able to make the logos line up across seams and zippers.

Caroline Dignes uses an airbrush to create the appearance of age and dirt on garments at the Santa Fe Opera.

A beaded skirt for *Shrek the Musical* sits on a table at Barbara Matera Ltd.

SPARKLE AND TEXTURE—BEAD MANAGER POLLY ISHAM KINNEY

Polly Isham Kinney is the Bead Room Manager at Barbara Matera Ltd. in New York City, a costume shop known for its exquisite bead-work. Originally the late founder Barbara Matera herself was the bead designer. She created pieces for stage and film, and the shop proudly displays a photo of her inaugural gown for First Lady Hillary Clinton, encrusted with variegated shimmery beads. As Kinney rec-ollects, when she started work at Matera's as a first hand, "I was very lucky in that I could draw, and pretty quickly they found that out, so I did Barbara's graphics through the years for her beading designs . . . I would do the drawings, and then she would interpret them into beads. I learned a lot just watching her do that. She was just brilliant, and thought of just the craziest stuff to do. I am not as good as she was," she says modestly. "I can put beads together well, but she would think up even crazier things."

According to Kinney, a good bead design for stage has to be full of variety so that it is interesting from far away. "It has to be bal-anced . . . and I like to try and do different kinds of techniques, use different materials on things." Kinney is not happy about the recent trend toward iron-on jewels. Unfortunately, very few shops have the time or skill for the precise handwork beading requires. "Hotfix [iron-on rhinestones] is easy. I don't think it's inexpensive, but it doesn't require a skilled crochet beader or hand-embroiderer. Anybody can hotfix, and it's boring. And if you see a costume onstage you can spot it, like that. It's flatter, and the shine is the same on everything."

Kinney enjoys when working with designers on projects gives her a chance to suggest embellishment ideas they might not have thought of. "Usually [designers] give us some kind of drawing with scribbles or dots or something and you say, 'is that beading?' hoping that it might be. Sometimes people pipe in and say 'it's hot-fix' and then you have to steer them in the other direction," she says, smiling. For *The Nutcracker*, designer Richard Hudson showed her a sketch of a male dancer wearing armbands. It was "just a line drawing of ovals, so we asked him what it was and he said jewelry. So that gives you lots of ideas then! We're going to do a combination of crochet beading and sew-on jewels." In most cases, she adapts the designer's original sketch to create a precise layout that fits the size and shape of the garment's actual pattern pieces. She also works out a diagram that shows the beaders where to place the different colors and textures.

Polly Isham Kinney works on a beading sample for *The Nutcracker*. A beading diagram for the front of Clara's bodice is visible on the left.

Josephine Spano attaches beads with the crochet method for *The Lion King*.

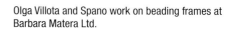

Olga Villota and Spano work on beading frames at Barbara Matera Ltd.

Close-up of Villota's beading frame.

Kinney credits the illustrations in a Sleeping Beauty storybook for sparking her childhood interest in costumes. The interest passed, though, and she applied to college hoping to be a large-animal veterinarian. However, her petite size and gender both worked against her. Typically for the 1960s, she was made to feel that women were not very welcome in such a field. She pondered what to study instead, and since she excelled at drawing, she decided to major in art and theater. For graduate school, she chose costume design. "The whole theater thing was a lot of fun because it's a very collaborative group. Whereas if you're a painter, it's very isolated." After receiving her MFA at the University of Iowa, Kinney taught costume design for ten years at a small college in Iowa, but eventually she wanted to join a larger pond and try her hand at professional theater. She moved to New York and set her sights on working with top milliner Woody Shelp. Three years in, Shelp's shop hit a slow point when some projects got canceled, and Kinney moved on. After a very brief stint making hats for fashion, which was "very chemically and very hot and steamy," she approached Barbara Matera for a job. She started out making trims, but soon moved over to first hand. Eventually, she became the go-to bead expert.

Although Kinney herself trained as a costume designer, when she maps out a beading layout, she takes her inspiration from the designer's sketch and concepts. "I hate to use the term 'beading designer' for myself because the designers are the designers and we go from what they give me, even if it's just a little line drawing and a discussion." When Kinney met with designer Tim Hatley about the embellishments for *Shrek, the Musical*, he requested "wacko" beading. For Kinney, this meant trying to go beyond the norm, finding unusual and highly theatrical treatments. For the Sugarplum Fairy costume, she supplemented the painted-on designs with discs of metallic leather, used both flat and like giant sequins. She surrounded the leather with touches of beading and also sprinkled jewels on top of the leather to give it more dimension. Kinney noticed that the sketch for the Witch included spiders used as accents. She asked Hatley with a twinkle in her eye whether those were beaded spiders. He agreed to her scheme, and after some samples, they settled on dimensional brooch-like critters made of beads and wire. The spider on the bodice sits on a web also made of beading. The delicate strands of the web are actually two rows of beads. Although they are all colorful hues, Kinney used darker tones on the second row to serve as a drop-shadow, helping the thin lines to show up onstage.

Costumes need to bridge the distance from stage to audience, and rich surfaces serve this goal. The vibrant textures formed by beading, paint, or appliqués make the creations shimmery and ethereal, weathered and earthy, or simply larger than life. Some of the most iconic stage costumes owe a debt to their embellished surfaces, from the collaged green fabrics of Peter Pan's tunic to the colorful cartoony stripes of the slaves in *A Funny thing Happened on the way to the Forum* to the sparkle of *A Chorus Line*'s finale.

A beader works on a spider decoration for *Shrek the Musical*.

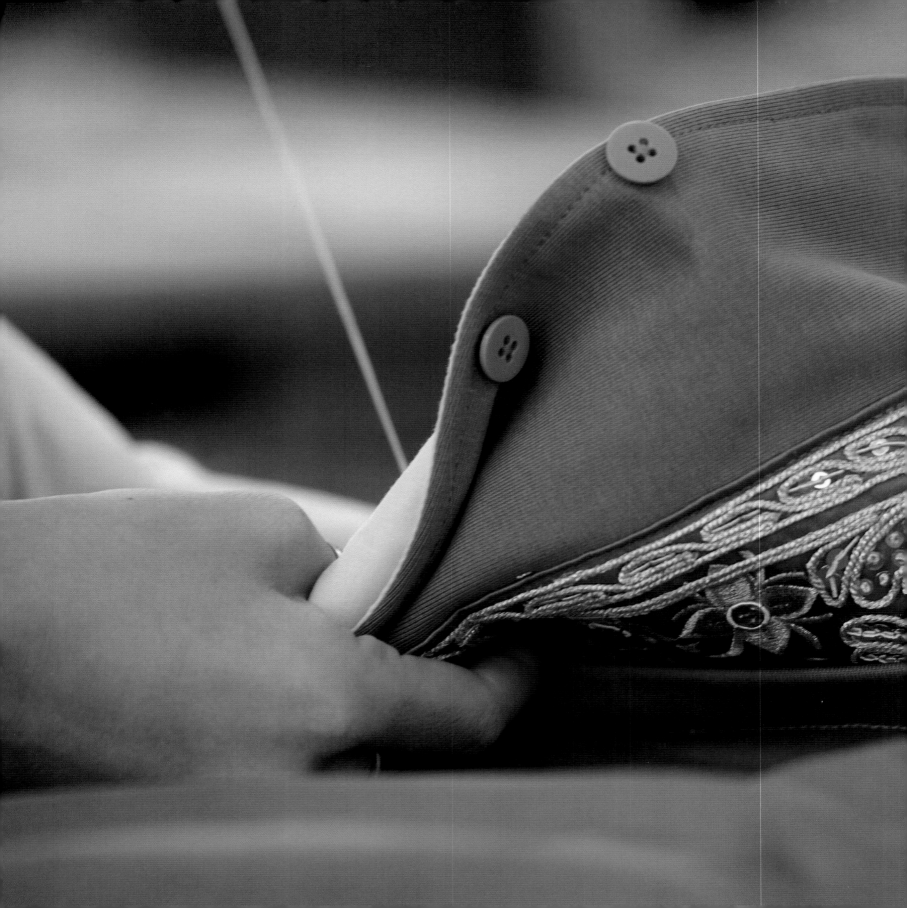

5

Construction

BUILDING THE GARMENT

The costume shop was doing a rush order around a famous musician's busy schedule, and he was due in for a fitting shortly. The draper met designer Adele Lutz in the fitting room, ready to try the first costume: a tracksuit embellished with painted flames. Meanwhile, her first hand finished the final assembly on the second outfit. The first hand looked nervously through the small pile of stretchy fabric shapes before her. While she knew how to easily recognize the curved top of a sleeve that gathers into an armhole, or tell left from right pant legs as they join to a waistband, this costume was a full body suit, including a full-faced hood. The pieces she had yet to finish assembling were cheeks and bridge of nose and forehead—not shapes commonly used by a costumer. While the final version would be painted to look like an anatomical chart of the body's muscles, the mock-up of plain white milliskin had no decoration to help orient the pieces. Trying not to panic, she instead looked for the small markings at the edges. Like any costume's pattern pieces, they had notch marks used to show alignment. She found the pieces that had mates, and then assumed the remainders had to be the centers: the nose, the chin, and the forehead. From there, she matched triple-notch to triple-notch, single to single, reminding herself that some edges shouldn't meet anything so there would be holes for eyes and mouth. Luckily the actual sewing didn't take long, as the pieces were so small, and she joined the head to the neck before David Byrne was ready to try his second costume.

A stitcher puts the finishing touches on a bullfighter jacket for *Carmen* at the Santa Fe Opera.

Above and opposite: Stitcher Emma Domingues at Parsons-Meares Ltd. in New York sews rows through layers of fabric to create a quilted texture.

Sewing is the most fundamental part of clothing construction. When the average person pictures clothing being made, they don't imagine fabric selection or patterning, they visualize someone using a sewing machine, joining pieces together. In actuality, the time sitting at the sewing machine is a fairly small part of the process. Once a person develops proficiency with an industrial sewing machine, which is a muscle car compared to the basic sedan of a home machine, sewing is fast. But, a stitcher's job also involves pinning pieces precisely together, ironing each seam after it is sewn, and binding edges of fabric so they don't unravel. The final finishing, done by hand, is of course time consuming as well. Attaching closures like hooks, buttons,

and snaps, securing dimensional trim like jewels and braid, finessing linings, and sewing delicate hems are all the job of the hand-finisher.

In university and many professional costume shops, the stitcher job is a learning position, and is closely supervised by the first hand. Stitcher is the entry-level position, and then workers progress to first hand (also called draper's assistant), and then to draper or pattern maker. In other professional shops, however, stitchers are equally skilled craftspeople and may stay in that position their whole careers. Drapers and first hands sew also if a project is on a tight timeline, but not with the same speed and accuracy as the full-time stitchers. Fine sewing is more than mechanically running fabric through the machine. Often the fabric

needs to be given a subtle tension to keep slippery fabric from shifting or coaxed into smoothly rounded shapes like the shoulder of a suit jacket. A stitcher with a good "hand" for fabric is much like a sculptor, forming the flat fabric into a precise three-dimensional shape.

The first hand's job, cutting fabric, also takes finesse and planning. The first hand ensures there are enough markings on the fabric pieces so that they can be correctly matched up during assembly. Small pencil or chalk marks called notches form a code to tell the stitcher which piece matches to which, and, on curved or stretchy areas, they provide calibration to be sure the shape does not become distorted. After tracing the pattern pieces, the first hand cuts them

out, adding the correct amount of extra fabric at each seam—enough to allow adjustability, but not so much that the inside of the garment becomes bulky. On printed fabric, the pattern pieces need to be laid out with care, either to match the design across seams, or to place the graphics of a large print strategically along the body. Should those large swirls be straight down the center of the jacket or offset? Should the darkest section of the print lie at the waist or at the hip? First hands also calculate how much fabric is needed for each garment, and coordinate logistics with the rest of the team—does the fabric need to be beaded or dyed before cutting? Do they need to save half a yard for the milliners to cover a matching hat?

Above and opposite: Costumer Quentin Desfray at work at Atelier Caraco Canezou in Paris.

COUTURE AND STAGE—
COSTUMER QUENTIN DESFRAY

Quentin Desfray stands at a cutting table in a sun-lit ground-floor workshop of the Atelier Caraco Canezou in Paris. He traces a series of long, narrow panels on sheer fabric, and then secures them with closely spaced pins so that the delicate surface does not shift as he cuts. A co-worker comes down from the second-floor studio and confirms that she was in fact supposed to cut six bodices from the fabric she holds in her hand. Upon hearing his affirmation, she nervously mentions that the fabric will only be enough for five. He sends her upstairs straightaway to confer with Claudine Lachaud, the boss.

Desfray grew up steeped in influences that would lead him to his chosen career. His mother danced ballet for the Paris Opera, and she and his grandmother were both serious seamstresses. Desfray began his six years of study in costume and fashion while in high school, and continued his training through college. His current job at Atelier Caraco Canezou is perfect for him, as the shop's reputation for finesse has brought them haute couture clients like Givenchy and Dior that supplement their stage construction work. "I wouldn't like to do just costumes or just fashion. The advantage here is that we do both. Stage work is great, but I love haute couture also. Fashion is more technical, more precise. The more complicated it is, the more I like it."

During college, an internship at an opera drew his focus to costume work. After he finished his studies, he went on to work for the prestigious operas at the Garnier Palace and the Bastille. Working as a stitcher, he appreciated when those at his level were included in the collaborative process. Whether or not that happened depended on the designer. At the Bastille Opera, Italian designer Franca Squarciapino created evening dresses for the large chorus in the *Lady of the Lake*. The designer came up with a modular plan to make five basic styles of dresses with variations so they would look like fifty completely different gowns. She used a wide range of fabrics, and worked directly with the stitchers to find different decorative treatments of jewels, lace, or ruffles for each dress.

He learned a lot at the "enormous" Bastille shop. He gravitated toward ballet work there, partly due to his exposure in childhood, and learned the traditional, labor-intensive methodology of tutu construction. That credential is what first brought him to Caraco, as no one in-house had the specialized training to properly stack the gravity-defying layers of netting. He has now been "nearly full-time" at Caraco for two and a half years, but is still technically freelance. He continues to work at the Bastille Opera from time to time, and for

other venues including the Moulin Rouge, Théâtre du Châtelet, and for films. Unlike the opera, where he works as a stitcher, his position at Caraco is as "costumer." While a select few of the employees do most of the patterning, the costumers do some as well. The costumers routinely adjust patterns, cut the fabric, construct garments, and also do the hand-finishing. The system is more project-based than in most shops, with one or several costumers taking responsibility for a given garment, and seeing it through all the steps of construction.

He appreciates the exacting standards he has learned from the owner of Caraco Canezou. "Claudine *hates* zippers," he says, smiling at the vehemence of his boss. "She is passionate about costume and she likes to keep things authentic. If it's lacing [in the time period]

it needs to be lacing." He recalls a couture wedding dress the shop made for an A-list celebrity client. The dress was all sheer lace, covered in beading. The shop spent two months joining the delicate pieces invisibly together, and adding all of the decoration. Most of the sewing had to be done by hand, and at times as many as eighteen stitchers were involved. One week before the deadline, Desfray melted a small hole with the iron in a layer of netting on the inside. They had to redo the whole back panel—even the most beautifully sewn patch would not suffice. A year later, the horror of the moment is still evident on his face. "But she got married—it's all good!" he says laughing. Clearly his talents far outweigh his mistake, as he is still a mainstay at the shop.

Costumer Manon LeGuen at Atelier Caraco hand sews a coat lining for an eighteenth-century opera.

Costumer Lucie Lecarpentier trims scales on a mermaid costume for a commercial event at Atelier Caraco.

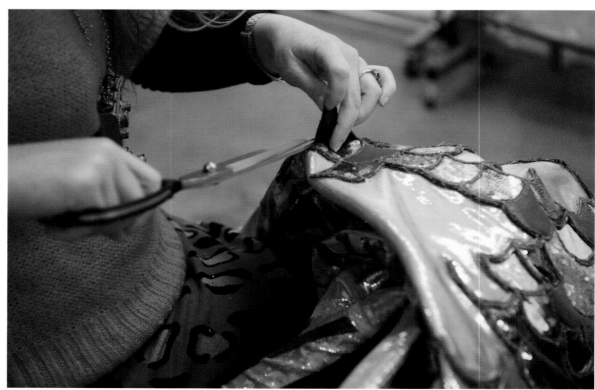

Lecarpentier moves the costume carefully so as not to disturb drying glue.

Above and opposite: Costumer Anne Blanchard at Mine Barral Vergez costume shop in Paris does delicate finishing on a beaded and feathered 1920s evening dress.

Stitcher Louisa Williams at Parsons-Meares, Ltd.

A LOVE OF SEWING—STITCHER
LOUISA WILLIAMS

Louisa Williams sits at her industrial sewing machine, a pile of fabric pieces to her left. The pins form a dashed line along one edge of the wool, adding a temporary sparkle. She takes the top bundle off the pile, nudges a lever with her knee to raise the machine's presser foot, and positions the corner of the bodice. The colored flecks in the fabric become a blur as the machine accelerates. Without varying her speed, she pulls the pins out as they come near the needle, and a smooth gray seam replaces the line they had formed.

Louisa Williams is a professional stitcher who works at Parsons-Meares, Ltd. in New York City. She has worked at the shop for twenty-six years. Williams started sewing at age sixteen, in her native Jamaica. She learned just because she loved to create clothing, but it quickly also became a way for her to earn money. She was a quick study, because as she puts it, "I took paper, and I cut patterns, and I started to sew. When I was seventeen years old I had a lot of work. I made bridal dresses, everything. I was gifted." At the age of twenty-nine, with her three small children in tow, Williams and her husband came to the United States to seek better opportunities. She first worked at Michael-Jon costumes and then Brooks Van Horn, one of the top shops at the time, but soon found a home at Parsons-Meares. Williams is grateful to the owner, Sally Ann Parsons, for her consideration over the years. "She never laid me off because I had kids, [which was crucial when] my husband and I separated. My two girls got a scholarship for college. I didn't have to pay a penny . . . You know, when you achieve something, you have to love the people who did it, who support you."

The good will that Williams has felt from the shop over the years is of course a two-way street. She is a lovely, upbeat person who always has a smile for a timid new hire, and her enthusiasm is contagious. During summer months, she often works with headsets on, listening to her beloved Yankees on the radio. Co-workers are occasionally startled by a cheer when the team scores. She glows when recounting the accomplishments of her children and her two grandsons but she also takes great pride in her own work. She loves seeing costumes she has constructed onstage, and saw her favorite, *Cats*, several times. She also has a great fondness for *The Lion King*. "I love *Cats*. I could close my eyes and do *Cats* . . . the textures, that beautiful painting. I love *Phantom* too, but *Cats* was my favorite." Williams had ample time to develop this love. Given that most costumes for *Cats* lasted only a few months due to the extreme athleticism of the actors, Parsons-Meares made a lot of body suits over the show's nearly twenty-year run on Broadway. Due to the custom painting, the costumes are tricky to construct. The spandex must be coaxed and eased to keep the textured designs perfectly lined up where the pieces join. Williams' work philosophy is simple, however. "I do it because I love to sew."

Valentina Abramova and Jacek Polak in the workroom at Barbara Matera Ltd. in New York.

Close-up of Polak, a tailor, at work.

Tailor Roma Dreizis at Barbara Matera Ltd.

Lord Farquaad's sleeve for *Shrek the Musical* at Parsons-Meares.

First Hand Ashley Rigg pressing a hem at the Santa Fe Opera.

PART OF THE PROCESS—FIRST HAND
ASHLEY RIGG

First Hand Ashley Rigg started in the performing arts as an opera singer. She got as far as her senior year of college and then she realized that she did not really like the lifestyle associated with performing. "I had no idea what to do—I had been singing since I was twelve," she recalls. She returned home, and was working at a restaurant and "one of my co-workers, a student at the local college, was volunteering at the costume shop and she just couldn't stop talking about it. And I thought 'I can do all those things!' I started sewing when I was very young, but it never occurred to me it was

something you could do and get paid. And so I went down to the school and talked to the people in the shop and decided that's what I should be doing." Rigg went back to college, and after a few years graduated with her new major. She worked for a while as a stitcher at the Cleveland Playhouse, and did some freelance design work. Then her career took a detour. Her father, who owned a drapery business in Florida, lost his workroom supervisor and Rigg went down to help out. "I missed the collaboration and it was a lot of rectangles—it wasn't as interesting for me." She drifted into a position selling advertising for a newspaper. After a time, "my boss handed me a brochure for the Florida Grand Opera—I was supposed to be

calling the marketing person." She could tell from the credits in the brochure that the opera was a large enough operation to have a fully staffed costume shop. "So I called the costume director, and two days later I had an interview and I was back in theater."

While Rigg had done some designing, she enjoyed it mainly as a means to have interesting things to build. "I want to have my hands in it," she says. She soon realized that if she wanted to work at the higher levels of the profession, she needed some more training. She went to North Carolina School of the Arts and received an MFA in costume technology. She is now continuing her training in the professional world, learning "more than one way to do things. From

grad school people tend to know just one way. The more you know the more valuable you are." She plans to move up to a draper position, and at some point to teach. This is her third season working at Santa Fe Opera. "I hope to keep coming back if I can find the right position. There aren't many summer places where the co-workers are of this caliber."

Rigg's favorite projects are ones where all those involved work seamlessly together. She recalls a production of *Into the Woods* during graduate school that gave the witch a mere nine seconds to change from ugly to glamorous, and the actress had to do it herself onstage. "Everyone involved in this had the right attitude. Everybody wanted

Stitcher Hali Hutchinson at the Santa Fe Opera.

Stitcher Ari Lebowitz at the Santa Fe Opera.

A close-up of an industrial serger sewing machine.

Edwin Schiff, Stitcher at the Santa Fe Opera, at the industrial iron.

A stitcher operates the foot pedal of an industrial sewing machine.

A stitcher rips out a seam to alter the fit of a dress.

to make it work and no one wanted to compromise the design, so everyone was really creative in coming up with their own little piece of the process—what can I do to work with you?" For her part, Rigg equipped the "ugly witch" dress with snaps along the shoulder, and then a zipper down the front, but offset from the center. The dress design happened to have a front panel whose edges featured a decorative band. Rigg turned these into flaps that made a perfect place to hide a zipper. "I feel like the audience is looking for something

to open at the front or back so if you conceal it it's more of a surprise." When the actress opened the dress, it had enough weight to fall to the floor, revealing the pretty dress underneath. She loosened the long train where it was tucked up, and with her other hand she pulled off her hat, which had mask and wig attached, and that was it. The builds were all completed in time for the actress to have ample time to practice, and eventually she got the change time down to four seconds.

Sewing fabric is in many ways the common link for costumers. From designers to drapers to craftspeople, most begin their careers by stitching. And, at the end of a production's build time, the final touches tend to be stitching. In a shop the day before dress rehearsal most likely everyone from the assistant shop manager to the draper to the dyer is sewing buttons and labels, finishing hems, and adding rows of lace.

Costumer Françoise Bianchi sewing at MBV costume shop in Paris.

Crafts and Millinery

CREATING ACCESSORIES

Just before dress rehearsals of the Broadway show *All Shook Up*, the creative team decided to rework one of the numbers, changing the chorus in "The Devil in Disguise" from nuns to ladies dressed for church. The choreographer wanted the women to wear little hats that would perch securely on their heads, but also be easy to take on and off during the dance. Although the orchestra would actually provide the sound, the church ladies would beat the hats as if they were tambourines. The milliner built some sturdy hats on a rush commission, flat-crowned with a small brim, reminiscent of tambourines. The designer, David C. Woolard, and the milliner deliberated on the best method to secure the headwear, and finally they decided to use magnets: one in the wig and one in the hat. They did a few trials to ensure they had enough magnet strength to hold, but not so much it pulled off the wig along with the hat. Since the project was on such a tight timeline, the desired hat decoration resembling bells or jingles had to be purchased; there was no time for a custom order. Although actual tambourine jingles at first seemed the obvious choice, they were too difficult to attach to the hats. The final solution was to buy brass discs at a scrap metal store that were thinner than the real jingles, and bend them like tacos. The milliners could then secure them to the hats by putting a strap of ribbon along the bend, giving the illusion of pairs of discs protruding from the hat. Odd, but all in a day's work for a theatrical accessories artisan.

Detail of a costume for *The Lion King* at Parsons-Meares in New York.

The workroom at Rodney Gordon Inc. in New York.

You can't sew it? It's not made of fabric? It must be the job of the crafts artisan. In a costume shop "crafts" is the catchall term for accessories and other nonstandard costume pieces: belts, jewelry, armor, masks, or wings. If a performer can wear it, it's a crafts item. If it's not worn, like a cane, umbrella or luggage, it falls under the purview of the properties department, which answers to the scenic designer. Depending on the size of the costume shop, one person may do the dyeing and fabric painting, and also make accessories and hats. Or, those jobs may be three separate positions. In large costume centers like New York, some costume shops do their specialty work in-house, while others subcontract to specialized businesses that create hats or shoes or dye and print fabric.

The field of crafts draws people who like to experiment. For standard items like cowboy chaps or Regency bonnets, artisans do use tried and true methods. But costume designers create new ideas constantly, and craftspeople must figure out a rubberized "bronze" wig for a statue, giant pretzels adorning a showgirl's hips, or a lion's head suspended above the actor's own. These artisans must know how to sew, and also how to sculpt, rivet, and solder. Sometimes they use real wood, fur, or metal, and other times they make faux versions from cheaper or lighter materials. Crafts artisans spend a lot of time solving logistical problems. They make belts that securely support a sword when an actor clambers over a rock wall, padded animal haunches that stretch as an actor leaps and dances, or a tiara that springs up when Cinderella removes her peasant headscarf. Just as the drapers do, crafts artisans create mock-ups to work out fit and scale before making the final version. However, instead of muslin, they make their rough drafts from paper, foam, wire, or found objects like plastic vases and cardboard boxes.

Although many of the techniques are the same as for making non-headwear, millinery is traditionally considered its own specialty. Milliners make hats from all sorts of materials, spiraling straw into sunhats, molding felt into fedoras, and covering structured bases with fabric to create satin bonnets and velvet top hats. Fantastical items may be built from anything and everything. Foam or wire can jut at any angle from the head, textured and embellished into show-girl tiaras or animal horns. Milliners fill drawers with stockpiles of plumes, silk flowers, ribbons, braid, and trimmings.

Milliner Rachel Navarro works on a top hat for *Wicked* at Rodney Gordon Inc.

Hat bases ready for coverings of paint or fabric on racks at Rodney Gordon Inc.

TESTING THE MOLDS—MILLINER ARNOLD LEVINE

Arnold Levine molds and smoothes a colorful plaid fabric around the contours of an oversized hat. Having ensured that the scale of the tall crown and broad brim provide the right degree of drama, he is now covering the shape. Rather like when upholstering furniture, milliners mold coverings precisely to the form. He adds the brim's covering and nudges the fabric as he pins it so the lines of color meet up with those on the crown. The finishing touches will be a band of ribbon, and an Arnold S. Levine label in the lining.

Arnold S. Levine, Inc. in New York's Garment District is best known for millinery, although the studio also creates masks and other crafts items for theater, opera, ballet, and film. Past work ranges from pastel flapper hats for *Thoroughly Modern Millie* on Broadway to a pickle costume for the movie *Jerry Maguire*. Like many costume technicians, owner Arnold Levine originally trained in costume design. He began his career as a freelance costumer taking both design and construction positions, including millinery. He had moved to principally designing, but during a slow period, he went back to millinery jobs. Grace Costumes offered him a workspace in their shop "and I thought OK, we'll do this for a little bit of time,

Bristow's colleagues customized her cast,
a souvenir of a mishap on her day off.

Wooden hat blocks, which serve as molds for shaping hats, on a shelf at Arnold S. Levine, Inc. in New York.

and then . . . that was about twenty-five years ago," he says with a smile. Although Levine continued to design from time to time, he has been happy concentrating on fabrication. "It's three-dimensional sculpture, which I really like, but it's still theater. I'm drawn to that combination of sculpture and history and design."

Since Levine now has his own studio space, he relies on the designer to give him the context he needs to be sure the hat coordinates with the rest of the costume. Despite his own training in design, Levine never tries to second-guess his clients. If a shape seems wrong for a time period, or if a color choice seems odd, he understands that among the rest of the costumes for the show it can make sense. "One

of the nice things about having been a designer is it means we are speaking with the same vocabulary, and that's important." Levine enjoys the challenge of interpreting a designer's sketch. He is proud when a designer says, "Oh, *that's* what I meant? OK!" He recalls a project where the sketch had a loose watercolor style, and in addition to making the hat, his artisans, on their own initiative, reproduced the painted effect "using three different colors of netting twisted together . . . and when we sewed the net we added little tiny beads." The designer was charmed by their attention to detail.

For Levine, the mock-up is an essential part of the conversation with a designer, and new products like thermoplastics (heat-activated

Finished hats and a wooden head block at Arnold S. Levine, Inc.

Wilberth Gonzales, Craft Artisan at the Santa Fe Opera, finds just the right shade of paint.

Shoes painted with faux aging dry outside at the Santa Fe Opera.

plastic) can make the trial stage simpler. When the finished hat is straw or felt molded on a form, milliners can quickly and easily mold a sample from Fosshape, a felt-like material that handles easily and hardens when steamed. A sample version of a hat that can actually be worn is key because it is difficult for a designer to judge the shape from a solid hat block sitting on a table. Unlike clothing, which fits in a designated way on the body, many hats can be worn at a variety of angles. Levine recalls a recent example where "we looked at the block and we thought it did one thing, but then you put the hat on your head, and . . . as soon as you move it back to get it out of the line of the face, then all of a sudden it wasn't 1930s any more, it looked 50s." However, since the actress was in the chorus, the designer decided she didn't mind a little face shadow, and kept her intended 1930s look by having the actress wear the hat tipped forward.

DRILLING AND MELTING—THE CRAFTS DEPARTMENT AT PARSONS-MEARES, LTD.

Parsons-Meares costume shop in New York makes plenty of traditional clothing, but they specialize in unusual costumes. Together with the in-house paint and dye department, the craftspeople are able to conjure up anything from an ice-skating blue genie to a superhero covered in a swarm of bumblebees. "We don't strictly do dress-making . . . I mean everybody here [at Parsons] does more than dressmaking, but our department, we're always making all kinds of crazy things. We're always cutting and drilling and melting and sawing", explains Katrina D. Jeffries. One project that stands out in Jeffries' mind, even compared to the everyday unusual, was making a Tweedle Dum costume for *Shrek the Musical*. In addition to sculpting a structured body to give the character an egg-shaped

physique, Jeffries and her colleagues had to ensure the costume did not touch the actress' neck or shoulders, even when she danced. The actress was suffering from a back injury, caused by a past costume. The costumers devised an internal corset and brace, and to that riveted aluminum hoops that passed over the shoulders and kept the costume away from her. After numerous fittings, some of which were attended by the physical therapist, and endless adjustments to the balance and weight, they were able to make the costume function to the actress' satisfaction, and still look like the design that its creator Tim Hatley had intended.

Crafts artisans become dependent on materials not at all intended for the clothing industry. Before creating a mask they use dental alginate, which dentists use to mold teeth, to make a life cast of the performer's face. Costumers commonly shop in hardware stores for items like PVC pipe, large-size zip ties, and dryer hose. The artisans at Parsons-Meares use gray air conditioner foam to support many of their fantastical creations. The foam has the right degree of stiffness vs. flexibility, and because it has a lot of holes it is easy to sew through. Many other types of foam become perforated by sewing, and just tear apart. Carrie Love, a draper at the shop, explains that the foam "is kind of a funny material to work with because when we buy it, they sell it by filtration power, but what we need is thickness and density. Sometimes we order it and it's not exactly the thickness we're expecting because if it has the same filtration power, their normal clients are satisfied . . . It's not important to them how thick it is." However, for a costume an extra $\frac{1}{8}$" or $\frac{1}{4}$" can throw off a whole pattern, or a lower degree of density can prove too floppy to hold the desired shape.

Stitcher Corina Cabrera adds embellishments to a costume for *The Lion King* at Parsons-Meares.

Stitcher Miriam Cestoni attaches bamboo ribs to a costume for *The Lion King*.

A close-up of Cabrera's project.

Head Milliner Deborah Nash at the Santa Fe Opera creates a preliminary model of a headdress in preparation for a conversation with the designer.

HATS, HEADDRESSES, AND HELMETS— MILLINER DEBORAH NASH

Deborah Nash is fifteen years into her job at Arena Stage as a general craftsperson, charged with dyeing, hats, and other crafts. After a few years in this position, she took a break to hone her millinery skills at the Kensington Chelsea College in London. She studied with master craftspeople whose credits included creating hats for Queen Elizabeth II, and for the Harry Potter movies. Although she continues to practice all areas of crafts, she has made millinery a specialty, and has spent many summers as Head Milliner at the Santa Fe Opera. Nash began in theater at a performing arts high school, and then went to college for costume design. A few years after graduation, she applied to Arena

Stage hoping for a job either stitching or assisting designers, but they offered her a crafts position. Interested in working at the prestigious Washington, DC theater, she took the job anyway. At first she wasn't sure it was a good fit, but then "I did a couple of shows with a lot of hats: *The Women* and *Guys and Dolls*. I thought they were very cleverly designed and I was getting really excited about working on them. I realized that maybe design wasn't for me; maybe I was happy to stay on the crafts side. And, I would have a more steady income."

Due to the Santa Fe Opera's busy summer schedule, Nash began work on the hats for *Le Rossignol* before designer Fabio Toblini arrived in town for meetings. Despite the lack of communication, their modes of thinking turned out to be very much in sync. To tackle

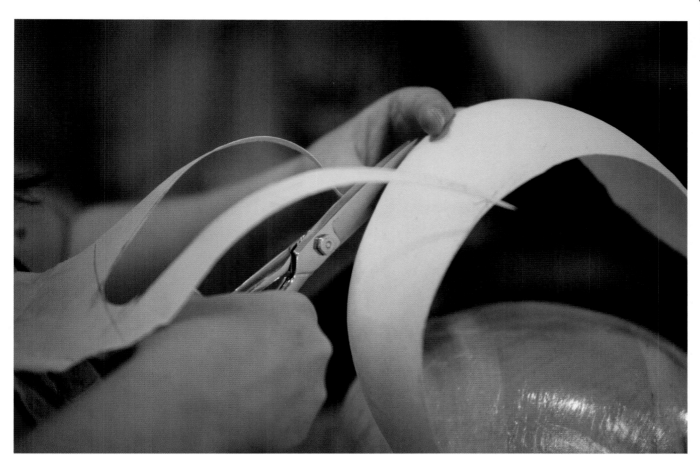

Nash cuts buckram,
a starched canvas material.

the unusual Mechanical Bird character, she studied the designer's sketch and then pored through the research he provided. She looked for an image of an authentic 1920s showgirl headdress with a good, stable base that followed the curving form of Toblini's design. She also had to devise a graceful way to keep the contraption securely on the dancer's head. One solution she thought of was to interpret the geometric bob the designer drew as part of the hat, rather than as a hairstyle. Nash recalls, "I wasn't sure if in his rendering he meant a hairstyle with a sharp bang and a spit curl, but when I was going through the opera's storage pulling hats for other shows I found a base that was buckram covered in leather, treated to look like a hairstyle. I showed that to him and it turned out that's exactly what he had in mind." To keep with the flashy, artificial look of the Mechanical Bird, and to contrast with the title character of the demure Nightingale, who is a "real" bird, Toblini chose to use plumes made of fabric, rather than real feathers. The millinery team experimented, creating samples using the fabrics in different ways.

They layered the colors in varying order, tried frayed and smooth edges, and different kinds of stitching around the central wire spine.

To create a covering for the mechanical bird's headdress that would match the rich gold velvet of her body suit, Nash decided that a paint treatment would work better than using the fabric from the costume. Trying to make the fabric smoothly hug all of the curves of the structure would call for unsightly seams and be difficult to attach. To figure out the best way to replicate the color and texture of the velvet, Nash's assistant Joanna Koefoed first made samples on a scrap of wonderflex, the same thermoplastic material she had shaped into the headdress itself. "I am doing [dimensional] layers with gesso and crystal gel for texture and some sawdust too, and also some flat layers with scumble [painted texture] overtop," Koefoed explained. "We will try both gold paint and gold leaf . . . and we will see what Fabio likes. I really enjoy being able to say 'I can do any of this—what would you like?'"

Assistant Milliner Joanna Koefoed shapes a base for the headdress.

Creating gold texture samples for the headdress.

Koefoed assembles a mock-up of a headdress for the Mechanical Bird in *Le Rossignol* at the Santa Fe Opera.

Designer Fabio Toblini's sketch for the Mechanical Bird.

Assistant Milliner John Ross Thomas snips threads on a hat mock-up.

Thomas and Nash remove a Spanish veil from a head block.

LEATHER AS A MEDIUM—CRAFTSMAN YANN BOULET

Yann Boulet peels back a layer of deep green fabric, leans over so his project is at eye level, and surveys the surface. He takes a small handful of springy gray fibers, pulls them into a thin layer, and adds it to the padding already in place. He replaces the fabric, and prepares to sew vertical channels along the whole piece. This elegant quilted doublet will be worn under a suit of armor to give the wearer extra protection from the enemy's blows, or from chafing. And, of course, the close-fitting coat also makes a striking fashion statement. Unlike most costumers who would just use batting, Boulet mixes in actual horsehair to help the padding retain resiliency. Plain batting flattens over time. Beside him, a young woman copies his technique on another piece, which will form the sleeve. Boulet finds her attempt

a little lumpy, and instructs her to distribute the padding more evenly.

Boulet is one of the co-owners of Les Vertugadins costume shop in Paris, where his specialty as a leather craftsman provides a distinctive niche for the small company. He has constructed armor, belts, helmets, and other accessories for opera, ballet, theater, and screen productions. The shop makes all kinds of garments from fabric as well, although they specialize in historical and fantasy costumes. This unique shop, which is actually a collective, also shares space with a photographer. Clients can rent historical outfits from Les Vertugadins' collection for fancy dress events, or have elegant portraits made on-site.

Boulet started in costumes as a hobbyist, teaching himself to make leather costume pieces for live action role-playing games. The fantasy games were a diversion while he studied for a degree in

A suit of leather armor at Les Vertugadins costume shop in Paris.

Craftsman Yann Boulet punches holes in suede before hand-sewing through the heavy layers.

Intern Julie Aymerich adds padding to a doublet.

Boulet at work.

literature. However, the "very intellectual, very literary" department felt increasingly static and his colleagues seemed dour and unenthusiastic. He questioned whether he would possibly want a career in such a field. He realized that he was more interested in making medieval cuirasses, and at the "late" age of twenty-five enrolled in art school to study costume production. He learned proper costume techniques for construction, tailoring, and patterning, which he was then able to combine with his leather-working knowledge.

He began his new career by working freelance, and then in 2012 joined Les Vertugadins. As part of his work at the shop, he mentors interns who need practical experience toward earning their college degrees. They learn not only the ins and outs of working with the leather itself, but also how to make the hard molded bases for the armor. Boulet is modest about his expertise. "It's a very specific technique, but it's no more difficult than a tailored suit coat or other techniques that my colleagues here know how to do."

Visual aids are a key element for communicating with designers. Boulet shows examples of his past work for reference before sculpting the base, to help ensure he creates just the right shape. For discussions about the surface treatment of the leather, Boulet keeps samples of different finishes and textures readily available. True to the funky style of the shop, they are within easy reach: hung on the bathroom walls. "At the office this would not happen. We are kind of iconoclasts. We don't wear ties to work," he says with a quick grin.

Crafts department head Brian Russman measures a performer for a glove at the Santa Fe Opera.

BUILDING MASKS, BUILDING RELATIONSHIPS— CRAFTSMAN BRIAN RUSSMAN

Brian Russman paces the concrete decking behind the Santa Fe Opera's costume shop. Casually attired in spotless madras shorts and fashionable glasses, he protects himself with a plastic bib apron and a respirator. The deck affords more space to spray, carve, and paint, and the mountain view is superb. Between adding coats of primer to his current sculpture project, he checks on the work of his crew. A young man paints an elegant pair of fuchsia lace-up boots to subdue them to a modest brown for a Belle Époque ingénue. Two others daub and sand a pile of shoes for victims of World War II, giving each the right touch of wear and tear.

Russman is working this summer as the Crafts Supervisor at Santa Fe Opera, his seventh season at the opera altogether, but his first since 1999. Russman explains that even before it became his chosen career path, crafts had always been "something that I gravitated towards.

I like the materials. I like making physical things. Part of what I liked about studying scenic design was making models . . . I can sew but my passion is creating things out of other things—jewelry making, masks, millinery." Now Russman is passing his skills along to the next generation. During the academic year he serves as Associate Professor of Costume Production at Carnegie Mellon University.

When Russman did his own studies in costume and scenic design, degrees in costume technology were new and unusual. After receiving his MFA from Ohio State, he stayed in the area doing design work. A few years later "on a whim" he applied for a crafts position at Playmaker's Repertory Company in North Carolina. He had had a few courses in craft techniques during graduate school, and he honed his skills on the job, following the adage of "fake it 'til you make it." His confidence grew rapidly once he saw that the designers at the theater were happy with his work, and valued his creative input. Seeking to further his career, he moved on to the Shakespeare Theatre

Russman working on a mask for *Le Rossignol*.

in Washington, DC, and then to New York. He first worked as a milliner, then moved to first hand and then shopper. Eventually through contacts from his time as a crafts artisan, he moved on to assisting. Russman accrued an impressive list of assistant and then associate costume design credits for Broadway and for film. Over time, however, he found that although his position was prestigious, he spent most of his time managing subordinates and coordinating budgets, and too little time being creative. He "felt like an accountant." He was still more drawn to making physical things, and he missed the collaboration between designer and artisan. And so, Russman left New York to train others in the hands-on skills he values. In the summertime he continues to work professionally, as a crafts supervisor.

"The best relationships are when we push each other—I mock something up and we have a conversation," Russman states. He prefers working with designers who involve him in the problem solving. "There are designers whose sketches leave no questions—you know what fabric it is and exactly how many beads it has on it. And then there are very gestural drawers—they don't know what it is but it was a reaction to a character or a script and you get to work together to figure it out." The solution usually comes from something simple but unexpected. He recalls making a stylized elephant head for *A Perfect Ganesh* at Playmaker's, a combination of elephant mask and gilded Indian-style headdress. The designer, Dona Granata, wanted the trunk to move. After a lot of brainstorming, the solution

Artisans use paint to age shoes at the Santa Fe Opera.

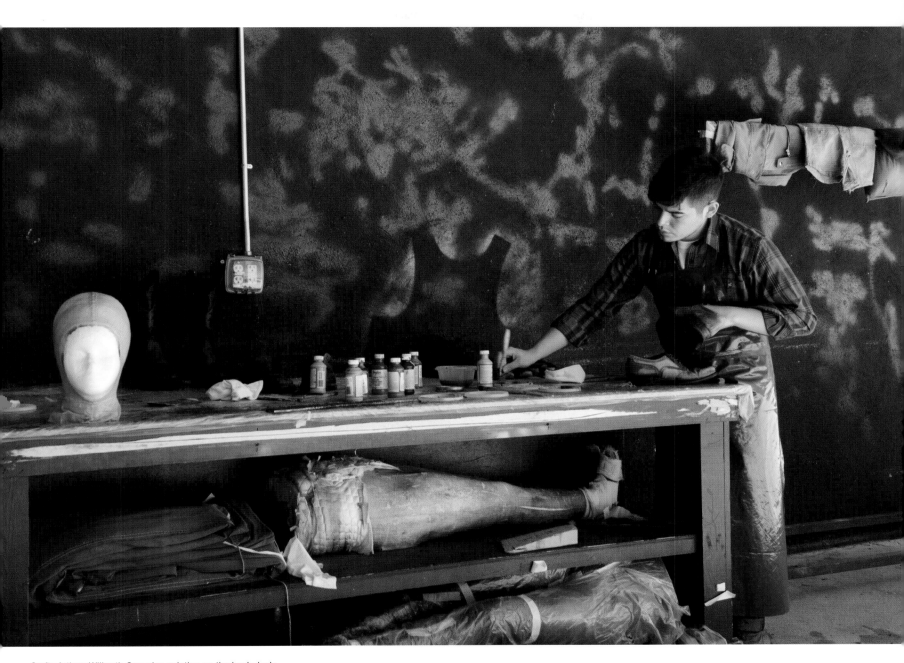

Crafts Artisan Wilberth Gonzales painting on the back deck.

Crafts Artisan Bryant Villasana paints a sculptural mask for *Le Rossignol*.

came from a necklace. The serpentine chain had the kind of sinuous movement the designer was hoping for, and the aesthetic of the tubular links echoed the rest of the headpiece.

A challenge from the current season at Santa Fe Opera has been the Envoys for the opera *Le Rossignol*. These characters, inspired by Japanese samurai, appear through a cutout high up in the scenery.

During the initial design meetings, scenic designer James Macnamara and costume designer Fabio Toblini jointly created the sculptural aesthetic. Suspended masks in geometric forms inspired by the artist Miro appear to be part of the decor until performers stand behind them. The fantastical Envoys from an exotic land deliver their message like human puppets, ensconced in a recessed window. Russman

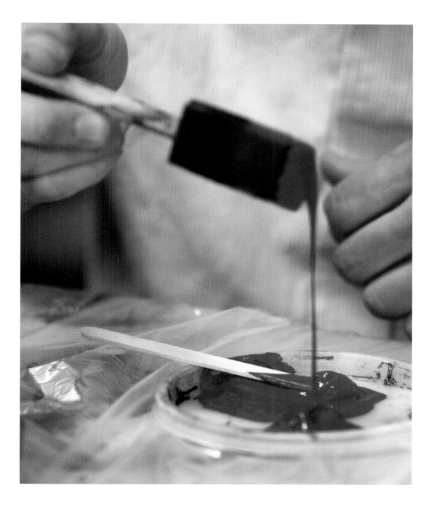

Artisans painting foam masks based on shapes from the artwork of Jean Miro, for the opera *Le Rossignol*, and adding color to shoes and details at the Santa Fe Opera.

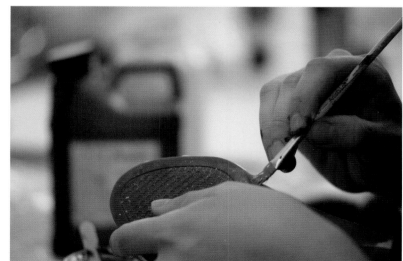

Russman and Designer Fabio Toblini discuss the shape of foam costume pieces for the Envoy characters in *Le Rossignol* as Aimee Deans and Deborah Nash look on.

and the millinery department created and fit mock-ups, as they would for any costume. But since the window was not much bigger than the three performers, the proportion had to be exact and so they performed the fitting on the actual scenery. Several technicians from the costume shop donned the helmets with elaborate paper plumage and the carved foam samurai pants, and posed in the elevated wooden frame on the opera's loading dock. The designers and director made sure that the three figures filled the frame without looking cramped, that they liked the effect, before the final versions of the elaborate pieces were painstakingly sculpted and finished.

Once the size and scale were set, Russman and his team were able to concentrate on the manufacture of the costumes. The structured tops were accordion pleated, supported by plastic tubes over the shoulders to hold the fabric in shape. The lower halves of the costumes were in fact not really clothing at all, but pieces carved from foam. The singers stand behind them, as if part of the still life. Russman and his team did the mock-up foam structures using several different decorative treatments, for the designer to choose his favorite.

Without the crafts artisans, a costume would be incomplete. Whether adding the right sparkle to the shoe, buckle to the belt, or crown to the head, accessories provide the punctuation that a costume needs. These alchemists who turn felt into gold and create animal life from foam consider the unusual a part of their daily routine. Whether the audience gasps at the shimmering angel wings, or remains unaware that the pregnancy is in fact padding, the crafts artisans have proved themselves an invaluable part of the show.

The stand-ins model the Envoy costumes on the scenery to make sure all three fit in the frame without looking crowded.

Villasana, Deans, and Thomas pose as stand-ins for the fitting.

7

Wigs and Hair

FINISHING THE LOOK

The Russell Miller Theater was presenting a musical based on O'Henry's well-known short story, *The Gift of the Magi*. Hair plays a crucial role in this tale of young lovers giving each other the perfect Christmas present. The young wife treasures her beautiful long hair, but in a selfless gesture, she sells it to buy a gift for her husband. Since the playwright graciously put the actual haircut offstage, the transition from a long to a short wig was fairly simple, albeit quick. The problem for the hair designer was how to style the wife's long wig, which she wore for the majority of the show. The narrative moved rapidly through episodic scenes set in a variety of locales; stores, streets, and scenes at home, where the husband makes a point of admiring his wife's long locks. In the circa 1900 era of the story, a woman would wear her hair up in public. However, if the audience did not see her long flowing locks at home, much of the production's dramatic impact would be lost. Pausing the action each time the wife needed a wig change would hinder the smooth flow the director desired for the production. Instead, the hair designer worked out a compromise hairstyle based on a turn of the century illustration the costume designer (the author) found. He styled the front of the hair in the soft pompadour bun of the era, but left the back down. To keep the hip-length hair from being too wild, he loosely braided it at the top but let the remainder release into a graceful corkscrew curl.

Micki Chomicki's studio at Any d'Avray Hair Designs.

Alexandra O'Reilly knots hair into a wig using a ventilating needle in the wig studio at the Santa Fe Opera.

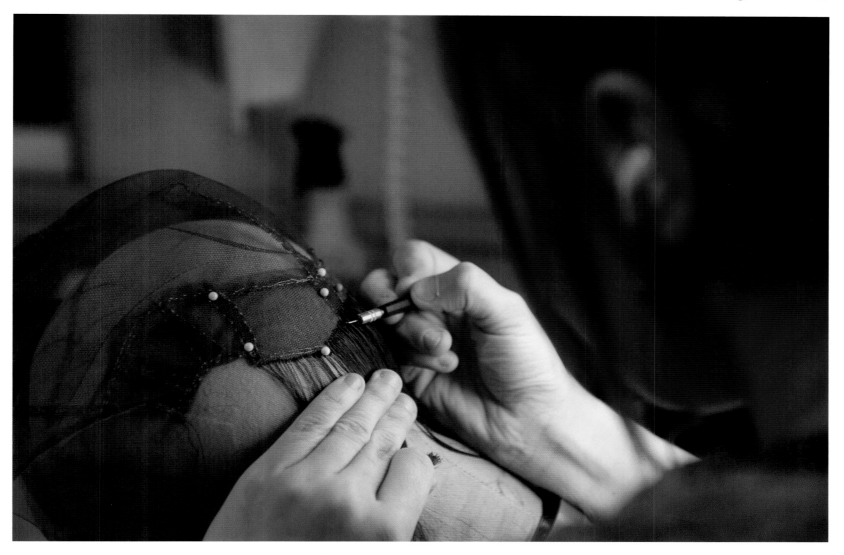

An artisan starts a new wig by adding the first row of hair to a custom head shape made of netting.

Wigs and hair are an independent department from the costume shop, but wig and hair designers work closely with costume designers to develop the total look for the performer. Particularly for period and fantasy productions, the transformation of the performer is incomplete without the hairstyle and facial hair. In most cases, the costume designer develops the take on the character first, and then the hair designer joins the process. Based on the costume designer's sketches and research, the hair designer creates a more detailed plan for the hairstyles for the show. These specialists also make suggestions to the costume designer about color, length, and style in terms of what might suit the performers, the period, or work well for the characterization.

One of the first decisions the hair designer makes for a show is whether to use the actors' own hair or to add wigs. For some productions it is all or nothing, for some it varies character by character. The reasons can range from artistic—perhaps the play's concept demands a highly theatrical look for everyone—to logistic—if a performer has to change looks quickly or needs longer hair or a thicker beard than nature provided. Decisions also are based on resources—both financial and manpower. Is there money to purchase good-quality wigs? Does the theater have a staff that can construct and maintain the needed hairstyles? The highest-budget productions use custom-made wigs, crafted to fit the head shape of each performer, and with

Finished wigs await styling.

each hair tied in by hand. These wigs are the most natural looking, and the highest quality. The mid-price option is to rent high-quality wigs from a custom theatrical wig company, or to buy good-quality fashion wigs made for the mass-market. Those with lesser resources make do with cheaper wigs, but stylists use a wealth of tricks to make these look better than they are, and even in small spaces they can work passably.

The work of a hair department includes making wigs and facial hairpieces, styling wigs, adding hairpieces or extensions to augment a performer's own locks, and gluing moustaches and beards to faces. They also style the performers' own hair, of course. Sometimes the choice to use a wig is based simply on keeping life easier for the performer. If a hairstyle is complicated or very time consuming it is much easier to walk in, pin up one's hair, and plop a wig on. Of course the hair crew also benefits by not having to do the style from scratch every day.

Sometimes the most difficult wigs are actually the simpler styles. A wealth of imperfections can be hidden under an elaborate arrangement of curls. A basic ponytail, which exposes the whole hairline, is one of the most difficult styles to make believable. A close-cropped style can be difficult over the bulk created by a performer's hidden long hair, or a microphone pack. (The norm for larger-venue musicals using forehead microphones is to put the mike packs in the wigs so the audience doesn't see cords snaking up the performers' necks.)

The process of actually creating a wig entails forming a mesh base tailored to the performer's head, and then adding in rows and rows of hair. Artisans use a tool shaped like a tiny crochet hook to tie just a few hairs in at a time, a process known as ventilating. The hairline is carefully shaped to be irregular, the soft short hairs a tad unruly. Often the wig artisans use multiple shades of hair to make the effect more natural. In most cases they build a custom wig with

Manuel Jacobo, Staff Artisan at the Santa Fe Opera, with a nearly finished wig.

real human hair, but sometimes they use synthetic, as the fibers can hold styles longer. After all the hair is attached, it is cut and styled. The wig designer works closely with the hair staff that will maintain the hairstyle daily during the run of the show. The backstage hair staff also helps the performers apply and take off the wigs.

ROTATING REPERTORY—DAVID ZIMMERMAN

David Zimmerman is Head of Wigs and Makeup at the Santa Fe Opera. He and his team are preparing wigs for five different operas with opening dates staggered over the span of a month. Today is a typically diverse day. Zimmerman meets with the designer of *Fidelio*, the third opera of the summer, going in detail through her sketches and her research of the opera's concentration-camp setting. Next he checks in with his staff who have been diligently tying hair at the counters edging the studio for some of the over thirty wigs they will construct this summer. Zimmerman's own hands are rarely idle: while discussing strategy with his deputy to prioritize

Stephanie Williams, Assistant Wig and Makeup Department Head, puts a wig cap on a performer to secure her hair before she tries on a wig.

the department's efforts over the coming week, he trims a grayish blonde bowl cut, upping the level of ridicule for an aging Romeo in *Don Pasquale*. He performs a hands-on check of the chignons several apprentices are styling for the chorus of *Carmen*, which begins dress rehearsals next week. Next he finesses the cascading curls of a wig for one of the leading ladies who has a costume fitting this afternoon.

Rather than working on Broadway, where the same show runs for months and even years, Zimmerman prefers the rotating repertory schedule of opera companies. "The thing about opera," he explains, "is that even though you are always going to do a *Bohème* and a

Figaro and a *Tosca*, they are different productions, they are different people. You are only doing six to twelve performances and then you go to something else." He divides his time during the year among several cities—Dallas, Santa Fe, and Philadelphia, supervising the opera's wig department in all three locales during rotating seasons. Although he briefly worked on Broadway, "the same thing eight times a week is really difficult for me."

While Zimmerman entered college planning to study voice and piano, he decided early on that performance was not in fact what he wanted to pursue, and switched to accounting. Later, while working in corporate administration, he was asked by a fellow church choir member to come help out backstage at an opera, applying body paint to the performers. The head of the department at the Dallas Opera saw both the interest and the talent Zimmerman exhibited, and suggested he seek an apprenticeship in Santa Fe. Zimmerman recalls "I asked him 'For what?' Because I had no idea that this was a career—I hadn't worked in theater, and as a voice major you don't really know." Zimmerman dove into his new career and didn't look back. After two years of apprenticeship, he was offered a position at the Metropolitan Opera in New York. There, he learned on the job under the supervision of hair designer Tom Watson, who at that time was also the head at Santa Fe. Over the years Zimmerman worked his way up, and now he is in charge at the two venues where he got his start, the Dallas Opera and the Santa Fe Opera.

Zimmerman enjoys working with costume designers, whatever their style of collaboration. He is happy when the designer gives him a lot of starting information, as long as his creativity is valued as well. But "sometimes it's also fun if they give you [a general idea of] what they are going for with their look and then say—well, just do something with that. And then let me just play." Zimmerman finds that communication is most successful when designers give him not only the sketches, but also research. "The problem is that most costume designers are really good at sketching the bodies and the clothes. Hair . . . eludes most of them, because it is not an easy thing to draw."

Research has played a key role in his current collaboration with designer Camille Assaf. This production of the opera *Fidelio* is set during World War II. A large percentage of the ensemble needs to look like prisoners in the concentration camps. The costume designer used research photos of actual victims, and chose an image to supplement each costume sketch. Zimmerman then had to translate the ideas into something workable for the cast that also preserved the designer's intent. He thought it would be easier to get the desired effect if they avoided shaved and extremely close-cropped styles on the chorus of women. The singers tend to have longer hair, and the amount of time it would take to get their hair smooth and skull-shaped under nearly bald wigs didn't seem a good use of resources. Assaf agreed. Instead, he explains, "a lot of the women in *Fidelio* are going to end up with some of my medium-length men's wigs and we will make them dirty and messy and look choppy and so that's how we will take care of that."

For the first show of the summer, *Carmen*, Zimmerman also felt very included in the creative process. He took his cues from the research and from the hairstyle shapes in the watercolor sketches. Designer Jorge Jara "had it all broken down by character. We'd talk about it and we'd work through [the designs] together. It's a process . . . some of it has come from me, some of it has come from him." Furthermore, since many of the costumes were assembled from vintage clothing and accessories, subtle shifts happened between the sketches and the finished costume. He kept in communication with Jara to ensure they were on the same page, and took cues from the preliminary fitting photos, which showed the singers in the actual costumes. From the pictures, he made adjustments like, "Oh, well they're a little seedier than we thought—maybe they should have some greasy stringy long hair."

In the job of a hair and wig designer, collaboration with the performers is at least as important as collaboration with the costume designer. Hairstylists spend a lot of time with performers and "any time you get that close to someone's head they have a lot of opinions and ideas." He adds smiling that "I also have to be a little bit of a therapist on occasion because . . . I'm like a really close-in bartender. I am literally ten inches from their face and you'd be surprised at the secrets you get when you get that close." Zimmerman feels that his background in performance and his understanding of the stress of being onstage give him an instant rapport with the singers. If a performer is not onboard with the hairstyle, he explains the reasoning behind the design choices. Taking the time for discussion gives the performers confidence in him, and ensures they understand "that I will never make them look bad unless it's deliberate." If he thinks a singer has a valid reason for requesting a change in a design, he will make the case to the costume designer or director. A good rapport also serves him well when he needs to persuade someone to go outside his or her comfort zone. A well-known mezzo-soprano he worked with who loves to be glamorous was playing a frumpy old maid character, complete with nerdy glasses. He bargained with her, since they had another upcoming show together. "She was going to be royalty and she said that she didn't mind if we do this [unglamorous look] here as long as I remembered next time she was the pretty one. And we did. She was one step away from a drag queen," he says impishly.

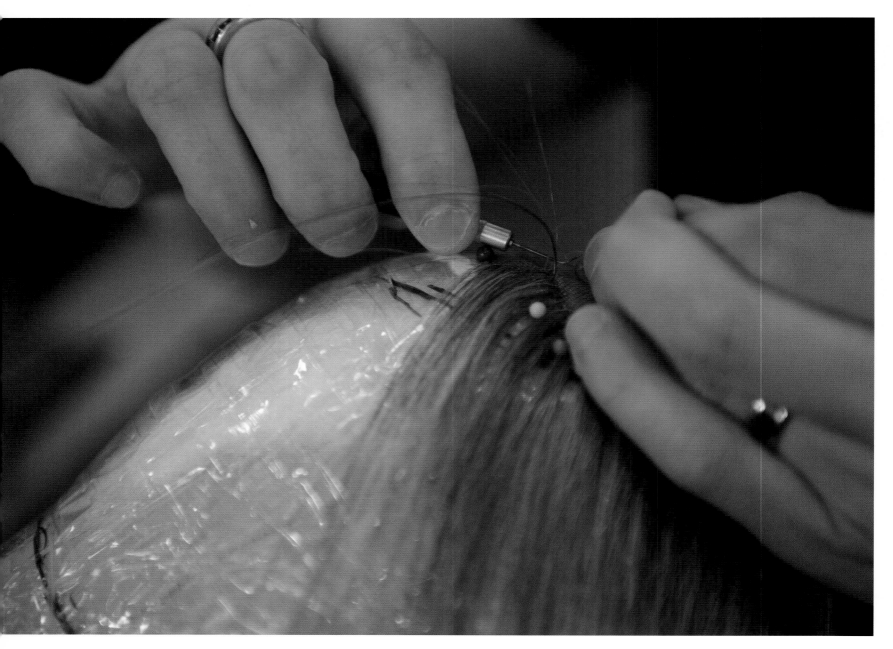

Varying shades of blonde are used to make a wig look more natural.

Ashley Robinson concentrating on her work.

Above and opposite: Carmen Mardelle, a worker at Any d'Avray, prepares hair custom-dyed to have dark roots. She detaches it from the binding at the top, and pulls it through the spikes to comb and organize it.

THE DANGER OF LIVE PERFORMANCE— CHRISTINE "MICKI" CHOMICKI

Christine "Micki" Chomicki clamps the canvas wig head to the end of her worktable, and carefully parts the strands of tousled brown hair until she finds the damaged section. Hairstylists for a music video, unused to handling quality wigs, have treated this one a bit too much like a real head of hair. While human-hair wigs can be brushed and styled, the delicate mesh anchoring the hair is much less forgiving than a human scalp. She threads a curved needle with a matching shade of brown, and closes up the wound like a surgeon. While she stitches, she glances across the room at an intern, who is

attempting her first solo project. The novice anchors a section of netting over the outline of a moustache. Chomicki comes over and runs her finger across it. She chastises the nervous girl that the netting is stretched too tightly, and the ventilating hook will tear it when she knots in the strands of hair. As the intern sadly removes the pins, Chomicki snags an espresso from her desk, and returns to her perch in the corner of the room.

Chomicki's work spans theater, opera, film, television, and fashion. She created wigs for a campaign for Chanel Number 5, and was "very honored" to be asked to restore a vintage wig complete with feathered headdress belonging to Jacqueline de Ribes for an upcoming exhibit

at the Metropolitan Museum's Costume Institute. Despite her evident pride in having such high-profile clients, her favorite projects are for live performance in any genre. She likes the "danger" of it, and the challenge of creating wigs and hairstyles that have to last through two hours of acting, dancing, and rapid changes. The logistical problem solving appeals to her, but she knows it must fade to the background onstage. "We try to be sure technical considerations never get in the way of the art."

Chomicki believes "the wig is the end of the costume, like punctuation," and so close collaboration with costume designers is integral to her own creative process. When Chomicki meets with costume designers, she asks them to explain their overall vision, even before showing the sketches and research. "I need them to tell me a story," she says simply. She prefers to work with designers who value her artistic contributions. "I don't want to just be a service. I like to be considered an artist on the same level." However, she has

also enjoyed projects with designers who decide every detail, such as fashion's Thierry Mugler. The technical challenge of realizing Mugler's intricate designs is enough to hold her interest. For any production, the clothing and wig have to create a coherent whole. She cannot judge her success without seeing the full effect, so she prefers to fit wigs on performers while they are in costume.

Chomicki first studied fine arts for three years at the school of Beaux Arts in Marseilles, where she gained a classical foundation in drawing and sculpture. Afterwards she went to makeup school, but not because of an interest in fashion or beauty. She was drawn to the character side of makeup, having "always wanted to transform people," and studied special effects. She worked successfully as a makeup artist for some years. As part of the job, she applied facial hair and wigs to her subjects, and became more and more interested in the craft. She visited wig studios, picked up the basics, and then taught herself from there.

Above and opposite: Micki Chomicki repairs a wig using a curved needle.

Chomicki currently runs the "Spectacle" (performance) division of Any d'Avray Hair Design, a high-end wig company based in Paris' chic Opéra District. While her department designs and creates wigs, hairpieces, and facial hair for a range of stage and screen projects, she considers large musicals her specialty. She just completed *Singing in the Rain* with costume designer Anthony Powell at Théâtre du Châtelet in Paris. For such projects, she pulls together a team of artisans who can create quality wigs on a tight schedule.

She likes the challenge of designing and coordinating over two hundred wigs. Choruses typically have at least twenty men and women, each playing multiple roles. When the actors leave the stage, they have very little time, often well under a minute, to change outfits and wigs. Chomicki and her pre-production team choose the wigs and create the initial styles, and then work closely with the team of stylists who will put the wigs on the performers, do changes, and maintain the looks throughout the run of the show.

Rising to a challenge is what keeps the business fresh for Chomicki. Her career goal is to continue to astound and surprise people. These challenges take many forms, from extreme realism to elaborate sculpture. One of the hardest projects she ever undertook was creating a wig for the French version of the reality show *Undercover Boss*. She had to disguise the subject so that he could go unnoticed by his

employees. While wigs for television and film are ready for camera close-ups, actual real life brings a whole other level of scrutiny. Adding to the difficulty was the fact that the "boss" had to be able to put the wig on unassisted, with no professional hair and makeup people on hand to finesse the look.

A memorable project at the other end of the spectrum was the operetta *Veronique* directed by actress Fanny Ardant at Théâtre du Châtelet. The costumes drew from the colorful 1950s style of Vincente Minnelli films, with an extravagant New Look silhouette. While discussing the designs, Ardant asked what hairstyle would complement the flamboyant vamp character of one of the women.

Without thinking, Chomicki muttered that she needed an Eiffel Tower. For a French hairstylist, an Eiffel Tower is a term for a tall, elaborate hairstyle. However, Ardant took her literally, and found the idea perfect. So, Chomicki had to swallow her chagrin and find a solution. She hired a model maker to sculpt a base for the tower in clear resin. Then, to more easily attach the hair, she covered it in netting to provide texture. She glued braids in an elaborate pattern to the surface. The four legs of the tower cupped the actress' head and held the heavy structure securely while she danced.

Chomicki looks across the studio as Margot
Arabian, a worker at Any d'Avray, prepares a
section of custom-dyed two-tone hair.

An intern pins netting over the outline of a
moustache on paper.

A close-up as Arabian uses a straightening iron to smooth the two-tone hair.

Hannah Wold, Associate Wig Builder at Custom Wig Company, trims netting and knots hair into a moustache.

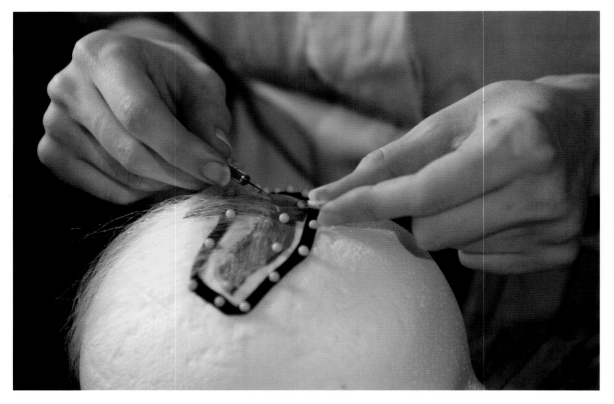

FINDING THE CONTEXT—HEATHER FLEMING

For Heather Fleming, wigs are a vital part of theater's storytelling. The choices that people make about their appearance and grooming tell a lot, and both the look and the function of the wig can help to convey personality, or further the meaning of a scene. She feels lucky to have worked for collaborative companies where she was able to make suggestions to designers, actors, and directors about using hairstyles to contribute to the success of the show. "I like that you make that connection with the actor and their character work in a really intimate and specific way." Just like with costume design, hair design must be geared to the specific person who will be in the role.

Although prep work for a show frequently happens before casting, "It's all theory until you get an actor."

Fleming honed her collaboration skills as the wig master for jam-packed seasons of repertory. While she roughs in the styles on wig heads, "I like to finalize the style on the actor. Of course it's going to need to be adjusted . . . Don't get attached to it until opening night!" She wants both the actor and the costume designer to feel comfortable giving input during the fitting. If the style is too finished, it's hard to make changes on the fly. The fitting is also a time to get actors comfortable with the idea that the wig is a tool they can use. While actors must respect the limitations of a wig, "if they can't

Above and opposite: Meredith Stein, Associate Wig Builder, takes a wig out of rollers and prepares to style a Regency era up-do.

behave with it like the character would behave with their own hair, then my work is too precious." Even a fitting can only get a wig's style partway to completion. After seeing the wig in context onstage, designers and directors often want changes, either to finesse visuals or to solve logistical issues that arise.

Often logical problem solving can lead to an interesting artistic idea. For a production of *Dracula* at Actors Theatre of Louisville, the creative team decided that the character of the doctor's assistant should have her hair down in the final scene where she is "bloody and damaged" to make it as dramatic as possible. They worked backwards to figure out when the hair of a properly dressed nineteenth-century woman might come down. They hit upon the idea of having the actor who played Dracula take the assistant's hair out of its bun during a previous scene, which created an interesting theatrical moment. In this era a woman wore her hair up in public, so "it was very sinister, and very violating, that he was taking this liberty with her person,"

Fleming explains. To make the bun unfurl dramatically, Fleming had to do some problem solving. First she had to work out the actual hairstyle that would look best for the actress and character. Luckily a simple bun was appropriate for a doctor's assistant, because for the moment to be dramatic and not comic the up-do had to be secured with as few pins as possible, but still stay up for most of the show. After some trials, she found it worked best if the actress discreetly pulled out a few pins in the scene just before. Fleming also had to decide the best way to roll and twist the hair so it fell smoothly. Next, "we had to teach the actor who was doing Dracula which pin to pull out when, and how to handle it so that it seemed deliberate."

Fleming became interested in costumes early, and during her undergraduate training she settled on the production side. She selected the University of Illinois for the costume technology masters program, planning on a career in draping, millinery, or crafts. By chance, she was assigned an assistantship in wigs. As she pursued the intensive

graduate courses, she realized that her sewing and draping abilities were not strong enough to make her viable in that profession. And, at the same time, she discovered that she both enjoyed and had an aptitude for wigs. During her first year of school, she learned under the university's full-time wig master. However, the wig master left the following year, and she was asked to run the department. "It was terrifying, but it was exciting too . . . so for me that cemented that this was what I wanted to do with my career." After graduate school, she took a position at the Barter Theatre in Virginia, and from there she became wig master at Actors Theatre of Louisville. She now runs her own wig styling company, and continues to work as a wig designer for several nearby theaters. She enjoys being a less noticeable member of the production team. In fact, she says that the best compliment she ever received was when the reviewer of a show questioned her wig design credit in the program, because he hadn't seen any wigs. Actually, there were four.

One of her proudest accomplishments was for another show at Actors Theatre: the yearly production of *A Christmas Carol*. The costume for the Ghost of Christmas Past presented "a trifecta—a quick change, a styling challenge, and a design challenge." The first hurdle was figuring out what the hairstyle should look like. The ghost wore a silvery unitard, which gave no reference to a time period or culture. Fleming had to figure out "what kind of hair does a formless spirit have?" She thought maybe the character could evoke Scrooge's mother. Although the audience would not explicitly realize this, the idea gave her a foundation.

She picked a hairstyle that suggested the late eighteenth century, and decided that silvery white would make a nice contrast with the actress' youth. The next wrinkle in the process was when the actress cast in the role turned out to have a circus background, and so the director added aerial silks into her performance. Suddenly, safety became a huge imperative. Fleming scaled down the size of

Above and opposite: Hannah Stoppel, Lead Wig Builder, puts the finishing touches on a loose, blonde style at Custom Wig Company. The pins help hold a wave in the perfect shape as it sets.

the hairdo, to be sure that nothing could throw off her balance or get tangled in the silks.

The next addition was a wireless microphone, to add a reverb effect into the actress' voice. For safety, the wire could not be exposed, which meant putting the mike pack into her wig. While this is a common place to put them, the wig needs to be built specifically to accommodate the battery pack. Fleming was too far along with the show to have either the time or the money to make a new wig. "Mike packs are only the size of a bar of soap but that's a lot to try to put into a head," she explains, so it had to attach to the outside of the wig, hidden in the bun. The pack also had to be easily accessible to the sound technicians, who check the batteries before every perfor-

mance, so its lodging could not be permanent. She attached a pocket securely to the wig, and added an extra piece with curls over it to ensure the square-edged lump was truly hidden. As a final complica-tion, the actress played other roles in the show, and had a very short time to get into wig, costume, and makeup for her ghost character. The backstage crew had to quickly secure the wig to the actress, but so well that even with the extra weight of the batteries it would stay on through all the flips and spins. They choreographed the change hairpin by hairpin, and Fleming added face-framing curls to hide the edge of the mesh, in case there was not time to glue it down perfectly to her forehead. Overall, "it was one of those things where this poor wig is having to do a lot of work, but it's totally worth it."

Wigs provide an important finishing touch to the character onstage, and a costume for the head. A short scruffy beard on Hamlet shows his growing distance from the court society; the blonde pixie cut on Maria keeps the novice nun attractive but wholesome. Perhaps even more than with costumes, when wigs are done well, they are imperceptible. And, if there is a problem, it can be incredibly distracting. A "wiggy" looking wig or a moustache coming unglued onstage can ruin a show like nothing else. Occasionally the hair gets to steal the scene, and then these artists show off their prowess constructing a towering beehive or an extravagantly twirled moustache.

Putting It All Together

CREATING A CHARACTER

The process of bringing a costume from sketch to finished product requires a team effort. To transform an actor into a character, each artisan works closely with the designer, but also with each other. Each artisan's unique viewpoint and set of skills complements the efforts of their colleagues. The final product becomes transformative, more than just the sum of the parts.

Here is a look at how the different departments work in concert to create one costume:

For the Santa Fe Opera's 2014 production of *Carmen*, costume designer Jorge Jara created a unique metaphorical image with his design for the Skeleton Dancer: a beautiful woman who is half flamenco dancer and half Day of the Dead skeleton. This figure of death foreshadows Carmen's fate. The build process for this one costume also demonstrates a typical collaboration in the costume shop.

A close-up of the Skeleton Dancer costume designed by Jorge Jara.

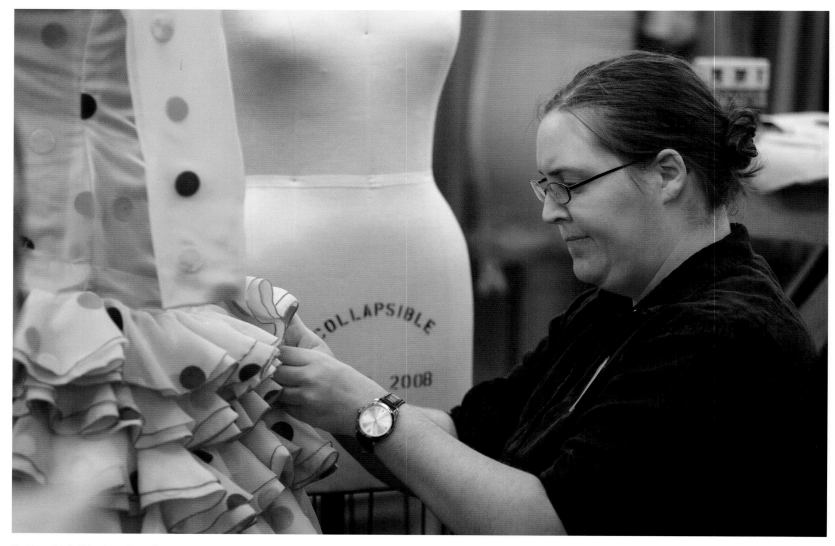

First Hand Beth Estervig makes adjustments to the costume.

Director Stephen Lawless decided to transpose the classic opera to a context more relevant to the local audience—the U.S.–Mexican border. The idea for the Skeleton Dancer grew from Jara's interest in Mexican culture, and the Day of the Dead celebrations. "It's a poetic way to show all the confusion of the heart visually: we see her from one side as a Spanish dancer, then she turns," the designer explained. He drew the idea of a half and half costume from Vaudeville traditions. He thought this dual idea would work well for a figure of death, and as the multilingual designer pointed out, the word for "death" is feminine in both Spanish and French. The dancer's yellow dotted dress is striking as she parades in profile before the bullfighters' procession. She then turns, revealing the figure of death that had been hidden from the audience.

To translate his sketch into reality, the designer had to locate the perfect fabrics. He found a print with the colors and scale that he wanted, but the flocked polka dots were on a background of sheer, drapey chiffon. Flamenco dresses need a stiffer, heavier fabric to function correctly, and so he found a bright yellow taffeta to use as a backing. For the body of the dress, the two fabrics functioned as a unit, but following the draper's suggestion, Jara chose to let the ruffles be two separate layers, which created more movement and drama. He initially planned that Santa Fe Opera's painters would

Costume Designer Jorge Jara.

create the graphic of the white bones on black stretch fabric for the skeleton side of the garment. However, by chance he came across preexisting artwork of a skeleton at a textile printing business while on another project in Europe, and thought it would save time and effort. He ordered two fronts and two backs to leave room for errors. Luckily, the height of the printed design was compatible with the actual actress, who had not yet been cast.

Having already had discussions with Jara as she built several other ruffled dresses for the same opera, draper Bineke Kiernan understood the aesthetic the designer wanted for the show. He sought to combine a mid-twentieth-century silhouette with flamenco styles, without being too tied to an exact decade or tradition. His sketch was clear, and the patterning for the skeleton half of the costume was straightforward—a full body suit, which costumers call a unitard. The draper's biggest challenge was engineering the two halves together. Kiernan had to balance the weight of the dress side so that it hung properly, and keep everything supported so that the centerlines were not pulled toward the heavier half. She actually built a whole unitard—one half made of the opaque black and white skeleton milliskin and the other made of nude-colored mesh. Beneath the unitard, she created a stretch corset to support the dress, and mounted a sturdy waistband beneath it. The skirt has only half a

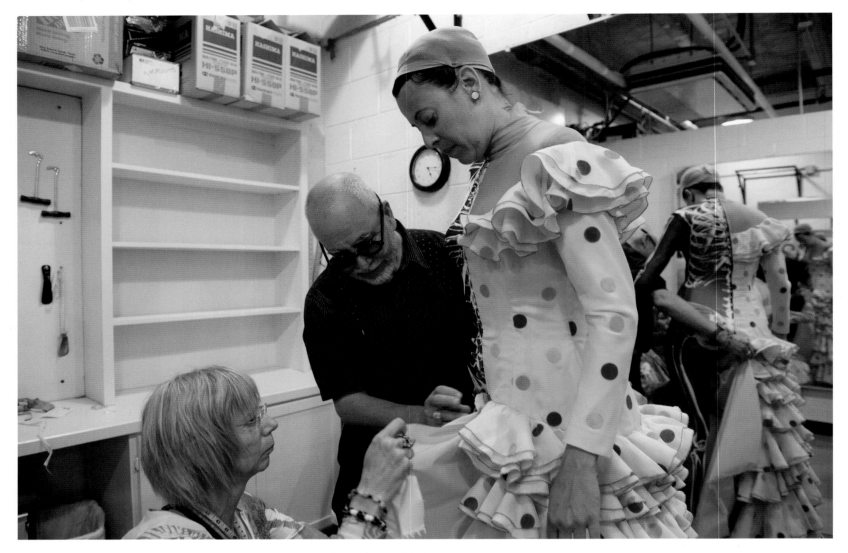

Draper Bineke Kiernan and Jara add a yellow panel to the skirt worn by performer Jasmine Quinsier.

waistband but it attaches through to this inner band. The bodice lies on top but does not actually support the weight of the skirt. Instead, the bodice attaches through the unitard to the corset, keeping everything even with the vertical center. A panel that passes between the dancer's legs connects the edges of the skirt from front to back. The designer had been very clear that he did not want the half-a-skirt to feel like a pant leg, so figuring out the best size and color for the panel became another challenge for Kiernan.

The performer, Jasmine Quinsier, played multiple characters in this production of *Carmen*, so she needed to be able to get into the Skeleton Dancer costume fairly quickly. The crafts and millinery

artisans suggested to Jara that most of the skull could be a pre-made and pre-painted surface, so only a small part of the dressing time would be needed for applying makeup. Joanna Koefoed, the assistant milliner at Santa Fe Opera, suggested combining stretch fabric and latex into what she describes as "kind of like a head prosthetic." A feathered edge of latex extends beyond the fabric to blend more subtly with the performer's face. "I had done a hood before with stretch fabric and latex but it didn't turn out as well as I wanted. I talked to David [Zimmerman, Wig and Makeup Department Head] about whether we could do a head wrap so it's really her head shape." Together they prepped and measured the performer's head

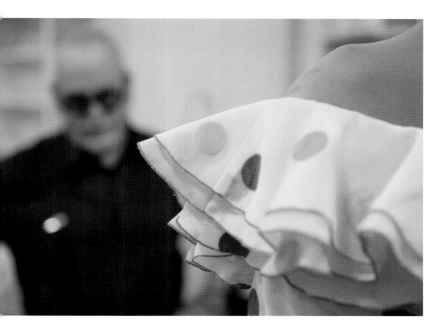

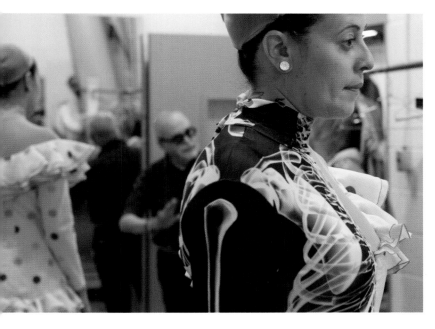

with her hair tightly secured under a wig cap so the fit could be as accurate as possible.

For the Skeleton Dancer's hood, the milliners made numerous samples with different kinds of stretch fabric and one, two, and three layers of latex, looking for the best combination of appearance and durability. The human side matched the performer's skin tone. For the skull side, the artisans painted white and black over the flesh-toned latex, matching the style of the printed bones on the body suit. Of course, no Spanish lady is complete without her mantilla, and so the millinery department's other contribution was creating a long black veil. A traditional tall decorative comb supports the long, trailing netting. However, its fastening had to be a little unorthodox. Half of the comb retained its teeth, which nestled securely into the wig. The other side snapped to the fabric of the latex and mesh skull.

The wig for the Skeleton Dancer was quite straightforward—a brunette shade compatible with Quinsier's own hair, styled in a bun to help support her mantilla. Except of course it took only half the time to ventilate, compared with a conventional wig! Zimmerman made sure that the stretch hood was left meshy in the spots where he needed to be able to pass pins through to secure it to the performer's own hair underneath the wig cap.

Jara added a necklace for the skeleton dancer, to help hide the transition between her head covering and her body. Assistant designer Sarah Bahr found several necklaces that could be engineered into one, knowing the designer liked costume pieces to be customized. The crafts department did the alterations and created a suitably dramatic choker in the exact width specified, complete with swags of beading and stones in the center. The designer had originally planned for the crafts department to create an elevated wedge to support the skeleton foot, since the human side would be in high heels. However, before they even started making prototypes, the elegant gold sandals arrived in the mail. When Jara saw them with the in-process costume, he decided that he liked the look as is. After all, she did have a full mantilla and a full choker, so why not a whole pair of shoes?

A large group of people gathers in the Santa Fe Opera's surprisingly small fitting room, each there to assess his or her part of the process. The mirrors on the two opposite sides reflect an endless chain of yellow dresses and black and white bones, along with draper Bineke Kiernan and first hand Lynne Kesilis, who busily check the fit of the bodice and the hang of the skirt. Jorge Jara and assistant designer Sarah Bahr discuss accessories. David Zimmerman pins the half-wig through the mesh of the hood into the dancer's pin curls below while Joanna Koefoed marks the latex hood with pins at the ear

Making adjustments to the latex hood.

Jara demonstrates as he discusses the veil and comb with milliner Deborah Nash.

Kiernan looks on as the wig is pinned in place.

Joanna Koefoed marks adjustments on the latex hood.

and pinches out some excess fullness. Head milliner Deborah Nash evaluates the drape and sweep of the mantilla. Wilberth Gonzales from the crafts department, who painted the skull on the latex, pops in to discuss the shading with the designer. Stitchers peek through the curtains, excited to see their handiwork on the performer.

As soon as Jara sees the costume on the dancer, he realizes that the black panel on the interior of the skirt is not going to work. While it does read as neutral, the skeleton leg disappears too much into it, and he is afraid it will not be visible onstage. He fetches a bolt of yellow fabric from the barrel in the shop and Kiernan and Kesilis pin a makeshift panel in place. Next the designer turns his attention to the dancer's neck. Zimmerman and Jara decide to switch to a fuller, curlier hairstyle to help hide joins in the costume. The assistant designer goes to the storeroom to pull a selection of fabric roses, so they can evaluate the full effect of the headpiece and the dress, complete with red accents at bosom and temple. None of the roses is quite the shape the designer would like, so they plan to refashion one to lay flatter to the dress. At the end of the fitting, everyone jots down notes, the actress is peeled out of hood and unitard, and she heads back to rehearsal. The artisans gather up their works in progress, and return to their worktables to finish up this one costume, as well as the hundreds of other pieces for the show.

Safety pins mark the location of the performer's ear.

Costumers interviewed in this book most commonly came to the field through a love of visual art, performing arts, or an affinity for making things by hand. The vast majority had been involved with the arts at a young age, on- or offstage, even if they envisioned themselves in other careers. Some passed from a childhood yen for fashion directly into studying clothing and designing or building it for the stage. Others took a more circuitous route, and performed onstage, studied social sciences, or even worked as accountants. However, the common thread in their stories is the urge to innovate and to discover, and the satisfaction derived from figuring things out. Both costume designers and costume artisans thrive on novelty. They search for better solutions to old problems and attack new ones with relish. They like to figure out the exact angle for a seam that will make a bodice most flattering, or the perfect tint of blue to make a scarf look like a morning sky. While an outsider may see some of their jobs as repetitive, the costumers focus on the aspects that are always in flux. Mixing dyes, tracing lines, or sewing buttons may stay the same, but the human element is ever changing. Be it challenging or frustrating, the costumers' canvas is the human body, and no two are alike. And, the group of colleagues exchanging ideas is also continually different. Each director's vision, dance number, or costume sketch begins a process that translates to new shapes, lines, colors, and textures. For costumers, the adage holds true that the best ideas are the ones where no one remembers whose idea it was.